300+

MOSAIC

TIPS, TECHNIQUES, TEMPLATES AND TRADE SECRETS

300+
MOSAIC
TIPS, TECHNIQUES, TEMPLATES AND TRADE SECRETS

BONNIE FITZGERALD

Trafalgar Square
North Pomfret, Vermont

A QUARTO BOOK

This edition first published in the United States of America in 2012 by Trafalgar Square Books, North Pomfret, Vermont 05053

Copyright © 2012 Quarto Inc.

Library of Congress Control Number: 2012934273

ISBN-13: 978-1-57076-556-8

QUAR.TTTM

Conceived, designed, and produced by
Quarto Publishing plc
The Old Brewery
6 Blundell Street
London N7 9BH

Project editor: Victoria Lyle
Content and copy editor: Claire Waite Brown
Art director: Caroline Guest
Designer: Tanya Goldsmith
Creative director: Moira Clinch
Publisher: Paul Carslake

Color Separation by Modern Age Repro House Ltd, Hong Kong
Printed by 1010 Printing International Ltd, China

10 9 8 7 6 5

Contents

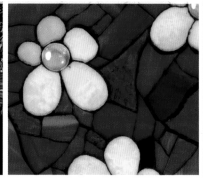  

Foreword

Mosaics are often described as craft and not an art form. I see mosaics as both. Mosaics are a balance of craftsmanship and artistic sensibility.

Mosaic art is unique in many ways. The reflective and tactile qualities found in mosaic materials offer a visual texture not found in other art forms. The Zen-like state of piecing the mosaic puzzle together is engaging, enchanting, and sometimes obsessive. There are many paths that bring people to make mosaics. I do it because I find joy in the process of making art.

This book is first and foremost a technical guide. It offers tips on design, materials, tools, and art projects. Beginner and intermediate mosaic artists will find the techniques discussed provide a strong foundation to creating mosaic art. The more experienced artist will appreciate the information provided about state-of-the-art adhesives, substrates, and fabrication tips. Following one of the step-by-step projects, using the templates, or savoring the beautiful examples of contemporary mosaic art work can be the spark to ignite your creative engine. This is a collection of tools, information, and resources to guide your passion for creative expression.

Mosaics can be a wonderful path for your creative spirit to follow. Continue your journey, or dare to take that first step!

Bonnie Fitzgerald

About this book

Aimed at all levels, this book includes over 300 tips, techniques, trade secrets, and templates that will enable you to achieve great results every time. The information is organized by topic and divided into five chapters:

1 Essential preparation

From preparing your work environment to the different types of tools, substrates, adhesives, and grouts available, this chapter presents a complete overview of what you will need to get started in working with mosaics.

2 All about tesserae

Covering everything you need to know about the building blocks of mosaic art, tesserae, this chapter explains the qualities of the most popular tesserae currently available as well as how to cut and lay them.

3 Research and plan your design

This chapter guides you through the process of creating your own mosaic, where to find inspiration, the process of planning and designing, and the principles of composition and color.

4 Working methods

Direct, double direct, or indirect reverse? This chapter demystifies the different ways in which you can lay mosaics by explaining the pros and cons of each method and illustrating the techniques with step-by-step examples.

5 Practical applications

This chapter explains how to successfully create mosaics that will be sited outdoors, and includes some practical and unusual outdoor ideas. It also guides you through the practicalities of framing and hanging your completed works. The book closes with inspirational examples of contemporary work.

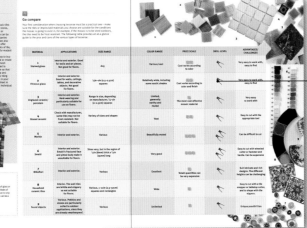

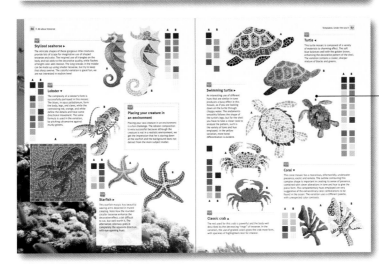

Tips
Information on all aspects of mosaic making from an experienced professional.

Fix it
Useful advice on how to avoid or rectify common mistakes.

Comparison tables
Provide an easy way of comparing materials to help you decide which is best for your project. The cost and skill level are shown on a scale of one to three, three being the most expensive/difficult.

Templates
Can be copied and used to make great beginners' pieces. Shown in two colorways, a palette of colors needed is given for both.

Projects
Explain and illustrate, step by step, how to create the finished piece, including a scaled template of the design and a list of all the tools and materials you will need.

Try it
Great ways of being creative with mosaic; these will inspire you to experiment in your own projects.

Jargon buster
Clearly explain key mosaic terms.

1

Essential preparation

Before you get started creating mosaics, take the time to set up a comfortable workspace that has everything you need within reach. Once you begin your work, you don't want your flow interrupted by having to go out and buy adhesive, or because you can't find the tesserae you need.

Plan your working environment

To ensure your mosaic-making is as enjoyable as possible, create a good working environment. The ideal is to have a workshop dedicated to mosaic-making. However, if this is not possible, you can set up a temporary workspace, clearing up at the end of each day or once you have completed a project.

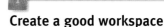

Create a good workspace

Whether your work area is permanent or not, it will need to meet certain basic requirements. Consider the points listed in the "ideal" workspace pictured opposite, and work out how you can meet these requirements in your own working area.

A good chair

If you spend long periods at the mosaic table, make your time there as comfortable as possible by investing in an office chair with an adjustable back and variable, supportive seat.

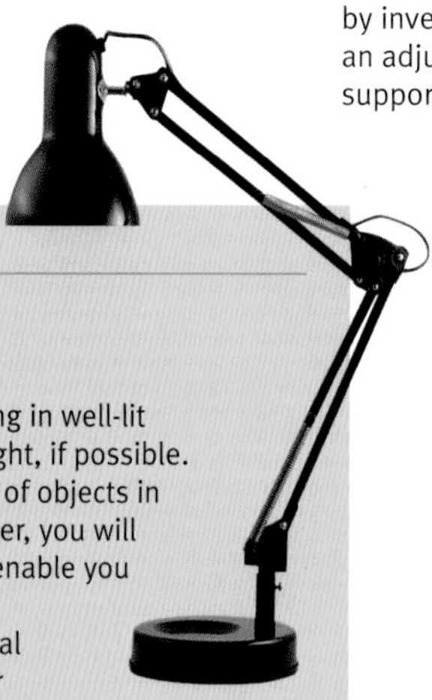

Supplementary light

Protect your eyes from strain by working in well-lit conditions with a good source of daylight, if possible. Natural light does not distort the color of objects in the way that electric light does. However, you will need a supplementary light source to enable you to work at different times of the day. A swing-arm lamp gives a good directional light that you can shine directly at your work. Combine this with the room's usual overhead light to reduce shadows being cast by your hands and tools as you work.

Color coordinate

The colors of your tesserae can often be inspiring, so it makes sense to have them on show in your workspace. Store your tiles in new or recycled glass or plastic jars, which allow you to see the colors at a glance. It is also helpful to arrange your materials by color, making it easy to find the perfect tone.

Get out more

If you have access to a yard or outdoor space, and the weather is fine, get outside to do messy jobs such as grouting or mixing cement.

> **JARGON BUSTER ◆ TESSERA**
>
> *The individual piece used in a mosaic—a mosaic is made up of many "tesserae."*

Ventilation (5)
Ventilation from an open window will expel the unpleasant fumes from some grouts and adhesives, and clear the fine dust formed when cutting tiles.

Good lighting (6)
Mosaic-making must take place in a well-lit area, ideally with natural light, and supplemented when necessary with electric light. You need to be sure your work can stand up to close scrutiny, and that any color decisions you make are based on an accurate impression.

Flooring (4)
The ideal flooring material is one that is hard and durable and can be easily cleaned, for example, with a dustpan and brush. If you work in a carpeted room, always put down a drop sheet before you begin, and vacuum the room when finished to clean up dust and shards of cut tesserae.

Shelves and jars (1)
Storing mosaic materials on shelves means you can easily see your supplies. Keep your tesserae in glass or plastic containers and plastic bags on a strong shelving system, since collections of tiles can be heavy. You can also keep powdered grout in lidded jars on these shelves.

Running water (2)
It is not essential to have a water supply in the room, but it certainly is useful to have one close at hand, because many mosaic-making processes require water.

Workbench (3)
Set up a strong, solid table that you can work comfortably at both sitting and standing.

6

Workspace safety dos & don'ts

Do

● Quarantine your work area so that tile offcuts and waste are not spread through your home, creating a hazard for children, pets, and other adults.

● Wear shoes that you only wear in the mosaic work area, to avoid treading shards of tile or grout into the rest of your living space.

● Keep all chemicals and additives secure and out of the reach of children.

● Protect your back by making sure that the height of your work surface and the chair or stool you use are set up correctly in relation to each other, so that you are not stooping or hunched while working.

● Keep a good first aid kit in your workspace.

● Always take safety precautions, even if you are only working for a short time.

● Clean up, lots. Since the raw material of mosaic is often sharp, never underestimate the ability of the edge of a cut—or even uncut—tile to inflict a nasty wound. Always keep your work area clean, sweeping up with a brush and dustpan—never with your hands. (And always keep some adhesive bandages handy to deal quickly with the inevitable nicks and cuts that you will acquire!)

Don't

● Work in an enclosed space. Ventilation is essential when using adhesives, mixing cement-based products, and cutting tesserae because of the chemicals and dust produced.

● Become complacent about safety as you get more experienced in mosaic-making. Even experienced mosaicists still suffer from splinters!

● Pick up the debris left after cutting tiles with your bare hands. Use a dustpan and brush every time.

● Let animals into a room where you are making a mosaic.

Tools of the trade

The tools you will need to make great mosaics include safety equipment, cutting and fixing tools, and pens, rulers, and paper for planning and designing. Don't be put off by the number of things you need, because some of them are everyday household objects and many are available from hardware stores. A few, however, will need to be sourced from mosaic suppliers, which are plentiful (see Resources, page 154).

Be safe

Always take note of safety precautions listed by the manufacturers of the products you work with, and wear appropriate safety equipment when working. The equipment detailed here is easily obtainable from hardware stores.

Safety glasses
Wear safety glasses to protect your eyes from shards of material that may be thrown up when cutting tesserae. If you already wear spectacles with reinforced plastic lenses, it is not generally necessary to take further precautions.

Filter mask
Always wear a mask when preparing ceramic and stone mosaic materials. If you sit in a sunny spot while cutting, you can see the amount of dust that is thrown up every time you fracture a tile. The dust from marble tiles is especially harmful. People who wear spectacles find it difficult to wear masks, because they tend to steam up. Try a variety of masks until you find one that does not have this effect. It is essential you wear a mask for mixing grout, adhesive, or anything containing cement.

Apron
Protect your clothing by wearing an apron in the mosaic workspace.

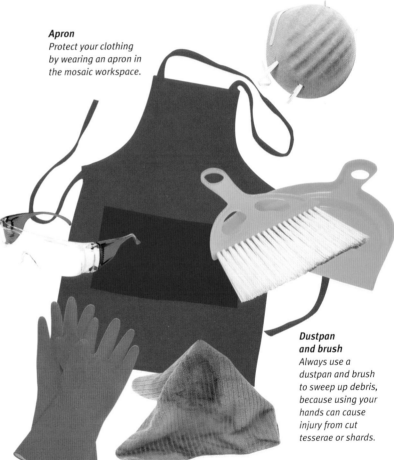

Dustpan and brush
Always use a dustpan and brush to sweep up debris, because using your hands can cause injury from cut tesserae or shards.

Rubber gloves
Cement or any substance containing cement is very harsh and drying for the skin. It is also a potential allergen. It is sensible to wear gloves whenever you use cement, cement-based adhesives, or grouts containing cement.

Paper towels and rags
Paper towels and rags for studio use should be absorbent and as free of lint as possible. Typical kitchen paper towels tend to have too much lint; instead use industrial-strength disposable paper towels that are available from most office-supply stores. Old T-shirts and towels make great polishing rags.

TRY IT

A finer glove
Instead of rubber gloves, you may find that surgical gloves, or those used in the catering industry, are more suited to detailed work, such as cutting and nibbling tesserae.

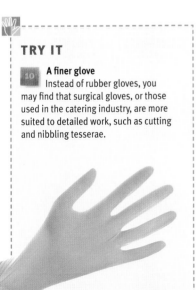

Planning and designing tools

The importance of designing and planning your mosaic in advance cannot be underestimated. Thinking about how your tesserae will flow (see About andamento, pages 52–55) and what the background will be, and transferring those ideas to paper will ensure the finished mosaic works. If planning on grouting, decide on the size of the grout lines and consider how that will impact the design. Good paper, pencils, and design equipment will make planning your mosaic easier and more enjoyable. Not all of the tools detailed here are necessary for the beginner, but as you tackle larger and more ambitious projects you will find uses for many of them.

Digital camera (1)
A digital camera is an invaluable tool in the mosaic workspace. Looking at photographs of your mosaic as you progress allows you to see objectively whether the design is working, and these progress photos can also inspire you to keep going. It is a good idea to use the camera to record color experiments.

Long-armed drawing compasses (2)
A pair of drawing compasses is useful for drawing accurate circles, and the long-armed version is essential for drawing large circles. Compasses are essential if you wish to draw fan designs (see pages 104–105).

Layout paper (3)
This is drawing paper that is thin enough to allow you to see through it, and is useful for working out designs. If, for instance, you have a design that is largely successful, but with some problematic elements, you can copy the elements you find satisfactory by placing a sheet of layout paper on top of the original drawing, and rework the areas that require further attention.

Colored pencils (4)
Select a range of colored pencils or crayons that represent the tile colors you plan to use. The more accurate you can make your preliminary drawing, the more useful it will be in solving potential problems.

Metal rule (5)
A long ruler is a fundamental workshop item, required for creating large mosaic templates and grids. Go for a metal rule, since this can also be used in combination with a craft knife or tile scorer to cut paper and score tiles.

Tracing paper (6)
This transparent paper comes in handy at various design and planning stages.

Craft knife (7)
Useful for everything from sharpening pencils to scraping off stray pieces of grout from your finished work, a craft knife used with a metal rule is also a more accurate choice than scissors when cutting straight lines.

Pencils (8)
It is useful to keep a variety of both hard and soft pencils. Soft pencils are easiest to use when developing a design, and hard ones are good when you need an accurate record of the final design.

Triangle or set square (9)
Use a triangle or set square to ensure grids for scaling and transferring your drawings are square and accurately measured.

Marking tiles

As well as marking your designs on paper and substrates, you will also sometimes need to mark cutting guidelines on your tiles. Good-quality felt- and fiber-tip pens (1) can be used for this, but make sure you use pens that contain water-soluble inks, so that any marks are removed when the piece is cleaned up after grouting.

A grease pencil (2) is another alternative, particularly useful on dark tiles. This pencil—also known as a chinagraph—has a solid, waxlike core that adheres to glossy surfaces.

TRY IT

Improvising compasses
If a pair of long-armed drawing compasses is beyond your budget, you can do a reasonable job with a long nail and a length of string with a pencil attached to it.

Get to grips with fixing equipment

Your tesserae are adhered to their substrate using the appropriate adhesive for the job, and many mosaics—although not all—are finished by the application of grout, pushed into the gaps between the tiles. Exactly what tools you use to apply adhesive and grout will depend on your choice of material, however some tools serve multiple purposes—for example, a good palette knife is useful for applying adhesive to your substrate, for back-buttering a tile, and for mixing grout. Most of the tools you will need are readily available and inexpensive.

Notched spreader (10) and trowel
Using the notched edges of these tools when spreading cement-based adhesives will help evenly spread and disperse the adhesive.

Grouting squeegee (11)
Some artists find using squeegees the easiest way to grout mosaics. The squeegee is very soft and pliable, so there is little chance of damaging the mosaic. Some squeegees also have a notched adhesive spreader that you can use when laying the tiles.

Grout float (12)
Grout floats work especially well when grouting ceramic tiles or flat mosaics. They consist of a spongy rubber pad attached to a U-shaped handle. The rubber pad prevents the float from catching the edge of a tile and cracking it. The float can also be used instead of a hammer to tap your mosaic into its setting bed.

Dry sponges (13)
An alternative to the squeegee is a small inexpensive sponge, which can be cut from larger household sponges and thrown away after grouting.

Palette knife
A palette knife with a flexible blade is useful for applying any cement-based adhesive or grout on a very small scale, or when working on a curved substrate.

Paintbrush and plastic spatula
PVA glue can be applied using a paintbrush or plastic spatula. For gluing, stiffer rather than softer bristles in a brush are best. A range of sizes can be useful, in particular, a fine brush for working on detailed areas. Plastic spatulas are cheap, widely available, and easy to clean.

Disposable wooden stick
Used for mixing adhesives and glues and cleaning out grout lines.

Sculpture and dental picks
These tools are great for pushing, scraping, and prying.

Sponge and cloth
It is imperative that you clean excess grout from the surface of your mosaic and you can use a sponge to do this. You can also buff the mosaic to finish with a dry, lint-free cloth.

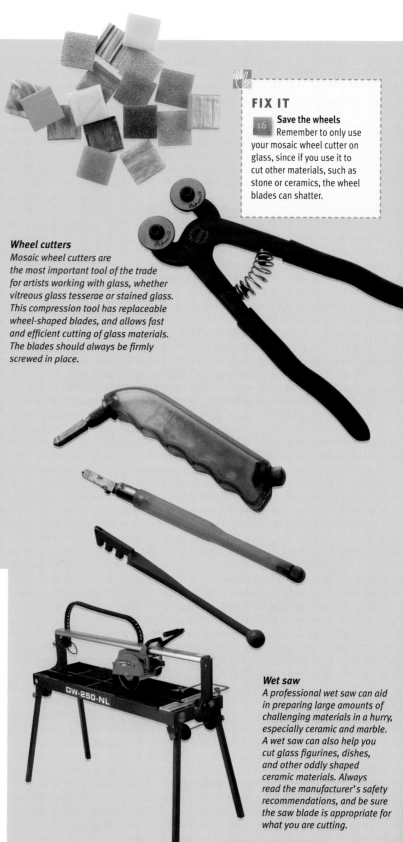

Know your cutting equipment

The cutting tools that a mosaic artist should use will depend on the type of material being cut. The initial investment is nominal, and you are encouraged to purchase the appropriate tools for the materials you choose to work in.

• To cut small stained-glass tesserae, use wheel cutters. To cut down larger sheets of glass, you will need a good-quality oil-carbide glass cutter.

• When working with vitreous glass tesserae, wheel cutters are the tool of choice. You can also use tile nippers, but care must be taken to ensure the tool does not shatter the glass.

• For ceramics, choose tile nippers, a tile scorer, a tabletop tile cutter, or, for large tiles, a wet saw.

• For stone, choose heavy-duty tile nippers, a hammer and hardie, or a wet saw with the appropriate blade installed.

FIX IT

Save the wheels
Remember to only use your mosaic wheel cutter on glass, since if you use it to cut other materials, such as stone or ceramics, the wheel blades can shatter.

Wheel cutters
Mosaic wheel cutters are the most important tool of the trade for artists working with glass, whether vitreous glass tesserae or stained glass. This compression tool has replaceable wheel-shaped blades, and allows fast and efficient cutting of glass materials. The blades should always be firmly screwed in place.

Oil-carbide glass cutter
If you find that you particularly enjoy working with stained glass, a good-quality oil-carbide glass cutter—which will last for years and is not very expensive—would make a wise buy. The two most popular types are the pencil-grip cutter or the fist-grip cutter. The cutter scores the glass, then a separate tool, a "runner," runs the score and is what actually breaks the glass.

Wet saw
A professional wet saw can aid in preparing large amounts of challenging materials in a hurry, especially ceramic and marble. A wet saw can also help you cut glass figurines, dishes, and other oddly shaped ceramic materials. Always read the manufacturer's safety recommendations, and be sure the saw blade is appropriate for what you are cutting.

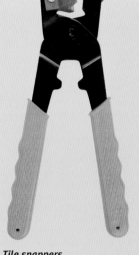

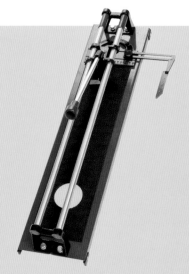

Tile nippers

This is the tool most suitable for cutting ceramic tesserae and household ceramic tiles. It is sometimes called a side biter because you grab the side of the tile with the nipper to cut. The spring allows you to operate the nipper with one hand, while you hold the tile in the other hand. Invest in good-quality nippers with tempered, well-aligned jaws, and keep the cutting edges clean by wiping off the glue and tile fragments that inevitably build up.

Tile snappers

Tile snappers have a scoring wheel and a snapping mechanism, and are useful for splitting vitreous glass and ceramic tesserae consistently and accurately into halves and quarters. Place a scored tile in the jaws of the tile snapper and squeeze firmly to cleanly break the tile in two.

Tile scorer

Obtainable from hardware stores, use this tool with a metal rule to score the surface of household ceramic tiles, then use tile snappers to break the tile along the line.

Tabletop tile cutter

Tabletop tile cutters are used by professional tilers to make light work of cutting household ceramic tiles, but if you work with household tiles a lot you could also use one to quickly split the large tiles into strips or large pieces. The lever of the cutter scores the tile with one movement, then you press down on either side to break the tile.

Hammer and hardie

Very precise cutting can be accomplished using the mosaic hammer and hardie, a device that has been used by mosaic artists for centuries for cutting stone and smalti. The hardie is a chiseled edge and is traditionally mounted in a log or piece of wood. To cut glass, the hammer should have a carbide-tipped edge; for stone and marble, the hammer should be steel. A combination hammer—with one edge for glass the other for stone—is available.

FIX IT

17 **Give the spring a helping hand**
Eventually the springs on a mosaic wheel cutter will wear and stretch, but you can help keep the grip tight by using an elastic band around the handles. The smaller grip is also easier on the hand.

18

From the garage

Any type of hammer can be useful for breaking up large household tiles or crockery into randomly shaped pieces. These shapes can be refined, if necessary, with the faithful tile nippers. To cut a substrate to size and prepare it for hanging, you will need a saw and drill. Make use of a carpenter's level to ensure you hang your work straight.

Consider your substrate

Choosing the appropriate substrate for your mosaic is essential and depends on the location it is to be displayed in—for example, inside or out, in the bathroom, bedroom, or garden—and the tesserae, adhesives, and laying technique you are using.

Choose a substrate

It is important to select the right substrate for the right application, and this guide should help you to do so. First decide whether you will be working directly (where the tesserae are fixed right-side up) or indirectly (where the tesserae are temporarily fixed right-side down onto a removable backing)—see chapter four (pages 112–129) for a more detailed description of these techniques. Then the key issues are whether the substrate will be exposed to water, if the mosaic is intended for interior or exterior display, and how much weight the substrate and the surface the mosaic will be attached to can support.

Wediboard (1)
This sturdy material—composed of Styrofoam encased in mesh and cement—is very lightweight and cuts easily with a utility knife. It is excellent for both interior and exterior mosaic artworks.

Hardie backer board (not shown)
This ¼in (0.5cm) no-mesh board product is produced using James Hardie's proprietary cement formulation. Hardie backer board is one of the most commonly used substrates for interior tile work, such as backsplashes.

Glass or Plexiglass (2)
As a substrate, glass and Plexiglass allow light to pass through the tesserae. Make sure you choose an appropriate thickness for your project. Plexiglass is a shatter-resistant alternative to glass.

Cement backer board (3)
This is a superior underlay for interior and exterior construction applications, including floors and showers. Traditionally it is made of Portland cement, alkaline-resistant fiberglass mesh, and lightweight aggregate. However, new to the market are these more eco-friendly versions made of a specially engineered combination of synthetic gypsum and cellulose fibers.

Medium-density fiberboard (MDF) (4)
Medium-density fiberboard (MDF) makes a good mosaic substrate because it provides a flat, stable surface and is fairly easy to cut with a saw. It is easily obtained from lumber suppliers and home-improvement stores. However, MDF is not waterproof, and will readily absorb moisture and warp out of shape. Therefore you should never use it for projects that you want to place outdoors, or for pieces that will be positioned in a damp environment, such as a bathroom.

MDF varies in thickness from approximately ⅛ to 1in (4 to 25mm). For most mosaic projects, MDF that is between ⅜ and ½in (8 and 10mm) should be adequate, but for larger pieces you may want to use something thicker.

Always wear a mask when you cut MDF, because although it has not been determined if harmful materials are released during cutting, the cutting process generates a good deal of dust.

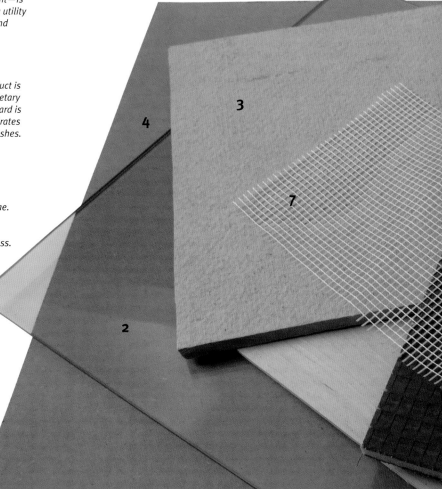

Plywood (5)
This is another good substrate for interior mosaic and is readily available. Marine ply can be used outside. However, this may be more difficult to find and you often have to purchase a whole sheet (4 x 8ft, 1.2 x 2.4m) instead of a piece in your desired size.

Aluminum honeycomb (6)
Aluminum honeycomb sandwiched between fiberglass epoxy faces, this product— created for the aerospace industry—is extremely strong, and can be used outdoors. It may be cost prohibitive, but is excellent for large-scale projects.

Concrete pavers
Any cast concrete object, easily found at garden stores, can be adorned with mosaic. Popular projects include birdbaths and cast benches. Concrete pavers make great stepping-stone substrates.

3-D objects
Terracotta pots are great objects to mosaic, but beware, they are not suitable for use in freeze/ thaw environments and cannot be left outside in those climates. However, they make wonderful substrates and you can use glass, ceramic, or found object tesserae. Just remember to bring them in before it snows.

20

Temporary surfaces

Double direct and indirect methods of working require the use of temporary surfaces, such as fiberglass mesh, face tape, and brown paper.

Fiberglass mesh (7 left and above) is used in the double direct method (see pages 117–121). It is specifically designed for interior and exterior mosaic tile installations and features resin-coated fibers to resist attack by alkalinity of mixtures containing Portland cement.

The face-tape double direct method (see pages 117–121) uses clear, adhesive-backed plastic as a temporary surface that holds the mosaic during transit and installation. Mosaic suppliers stock face tape—also known as tile or ceramic tape— or you can use clear contact paper or clear packing tape.

When working indirectly (see pages 124–129), the tesserae are temporarily stuck down on brown paper, before the whole mosaic is transported to its final site. You can buy brown paper in rolls for wrapping parcels, or from mosaic suppliers in precut sheets. Make sure your paper is not waxed or coated, because it will be resistant to absorbing moisture. Use a heavy grade of paper—42lb (160gsm) is ideal. Thinner papers do not take the weight of heavy mosaic materials as easily and are more likely to stretch. Thicker papers take a long time to absorb moisture when it is time to peel them off, and also have a tendency to peel off in layers.

21

Cut to size

Always cut your substrate to the correct size before beginning your mosaic—cutting the board along the edge of a line of tiles that has been glued down is almost impossible. The edge of the board is also a useful guide to keep tiles in straight lines. Use sandpaper to tidy up your saw cuts before you seal the board.

Mark up the board with a pencil and metal rule, making sure that all sides are parallel. (Some craft or hardware stores will cut rectangular boards from larger sheets for a small charge.)

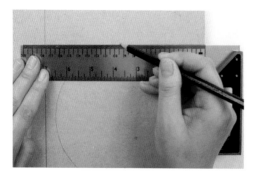

MDF can be cut to size with a conventional handsaw, a power circular saw, or a bandsaw.

To cut out decorative shapes and curves, you can also use an electric jigsaw. Make sure the board is supported properly while cutting it, and wear a dust mask at all times.

22

Prepare MDF

MDF is porous, and by applying a sealant you will be helping to create a mechanical bond. Apply either a paint primer or a 50:50 mix of PVA glue and water. If you are using glass as your tesserae, a white or pale-gray surface will keep the colors true.

24

Plan ahead

When preparing a substrate for a mosaic, plan in advance how you will finally mount it to the wall. It is always easier to install your hanging hardware before you begin working. With some substrates, such as Wediboard, it is nearly impossible to install hardware after the fact. See pages 144–147 for tips on hanging and mounting mosaics.

Predrill the board with the holes needed for your chosen method of mounting or hanging. By installing in advance, you also limit your chances of damaging your completed artwork. The board will be considerably heavier when covered with tesserae and grout, so use the empty substrate to mark up the wall for the relevant mounting screw holes. It is much easier to hold up the board before it is weighted down with your mosaic.

23

Broaden your horizons

Virtually any hard, sturdy object can become a mosaic substrate; it just needs to be properly prepared and appropriate adhesive used. Any surface that is porous must be sealed. A porous surface is full of tiny holes that allow fluids or gases to pass through, whereas nonporous surfaces do not allow anything to pass through or be absorbed.

TRY IT

Provide extra grip
Deep score lines in a wooden or MDF substrate give adhesives something extra to grip on to. Use a sharp craft knife to make scratches in the surface in a crisscross pattern, then seal with primer or a 50:50 PVA-water mix.

Predrill your board and install your chosen hanging equipment before you start work.

TYPE OF SUBSTRATE	INDOOR/ OUTDOOR	NECESSARY PREPARATION	TYPES OF ADHESIVE	PRICE SCALE	SKILL LEVEL	ADVANTAGES/ CHALLENGES
MDF and indoor-grade plywood	Indoor	50:50 PVA glue:water or paint primer	PVA glue, thinset	◼	✂	Easily available, easy to cut
Marine-grade plywood	Outdoor	Thinset skim coat	Thinset	◼◼◼	✂	Comes in large sheets from specialty lumber yards
Wediboard	Indoor/Outdoor	None	Indoor: PVA glue Outdoor: Thinset	◼◼	✂✂	Usually order online, will bow or break if mosaic is too heavy
Cement backer board	Indoor/Outdoor	None	Thinset	◼	✂✂	Easily available, need special saw blade to cut
Hardie backer board	Indoor and low water	None	Thinset, PVA glue	◼	✂✂	Easily available, need special tool or saw blade to cut
Glass	Indoor/ Outdoor (with appropriate adhesive)	50:50 PVA glue:water	PVA glue (indoor only), exterior-rated silicone adhesive, or MAC glue	◼	✂✂	Easily available, fragile
Plexiglass	Indoor	50:50 PVA glue:water	PVA glue, silicone adhesive, or MAC glue	◼◼	✂	Easily available, shatter resistant
Aluminum honeycomb	Indoor/Outdoor	Thinset skim coat	Thinset	◼◼◼	✂✂✂	Special order, perfect for very large installations
Concrete pavers and garden objects	Outdoor	None	Thinset	◼	✂	Easily available, you can mosaic anything that has a concerete base
Terracotta pottery	Outdoor, but not freeze-thaw safe	Concrete sealer	PVA, silicone, or MAC glue	◼	✂	Easily available

Adhesives and how to use them

Various kinds of adhesive are used for the different methods of making mosaics, and the adhesive you use depends on whether you are creating a mosaic for exterior use or interior display, your choice of tessarae, and if you are working directly or indirectly. Think about the characteristics of your adhesive and choose accordingly. Quick-setting adhesives might be useful if you are affixing to plaster or another material that should not have prolonged exposure to moisture. Some adhesives are better at sticking to wood than others. Some adhesives also have different sensitivities to temperature. A slow-setting adhesive is often the choice for outdoor siting. Always read the manufacturer's data to ascertain the suitability of various adhesives.

Common choices

The three most common types of adhesive used for fixing mosaics to a substrate before grouting are PVA glue, cement-based adhesives, and silicone adhesives.

PVA glue (1)

Ordinary PVA glue is used to directly lay mosaics (see pages 114–116) for indoor applications. It is suitable where at least one of the surfaces is porous—for example, glass tesserae on an MDF substrate. There are many manufacturers of PVA glue. A brand that has extra "body" to it—not a "school glue," which is a watered-down version—is recommended. These adhesives are water-based and clean up with soap and warm water. PVA is only toxic to ingest; it does not emit any harmful fumes, and is not hazardous to touch.

Thinset (2)

Thinset is the adhesive of choice for many mosaic artists working with materials that will not be grouted, materials that are not uniform in shape or size, or if the piece is intended for outdoor use. Thinset adhesive mortar is an organic substance made of Portland cement, silica, sand, and moisture-retaining agents. It is called thinset because it is a thin-setting bed—as opposed to a thick-setting bed used in construction. It is a cementitious product, meaning it has the bonding properties of concrete.

Thinset is available ready-mixed or in powdered form to be mixed with water or polymer additives. Make sure the product you buy is rated for your use, since not all thinset is suitable for exterior use. In the tile trade, thinset is often called "mud."

Silicone adhesive (3)

Silicone adhesive is a transparent, flexible, and watertight glue that is perfect where both surfaces are nonporous, such as glass on glass. It can be very sticky, but that is helpful when securing tesserae to vertical surfaces. Exterior-rated silicone, such as that labeled "for windows and doors," can also be used for most exterior applications.

Adhesive comparison table

Mosaics can last forever if you build them using the correct combination of materials. Your substrate choice must be appropriate for either interior or exterior use, if your work is for outside your tesserae must be rated appropriately for your climate, and, most importantly, your adhesive must be compatible with both. The table opposite provides an at-a-glance guide to the pros and cons of the various types of adhesives.

Please note that all adhesives should be left to fully dry for at least 24 hours before grouting.

> **JARGON BUSTER ◆ PVA**
> *Polyvinyl acetate (PVA) is a rubbery synthetic polymer and probably the most common adhesive on the market (also known as white craft glue).*

28

Other choices

As well as the three most common adhesive choices, the following may also be used.

• **Tile mastic**: This is a sticky adhesive that comes premixed. It works especially well on vertical surfaces and for tesserae of various thicknesses, such as dishes and crockery. It is not rated for floors, exterior applications, or very wet environments, but it is convenient and easy to use.

• **Epoxy glue**: This is a very strong two-part adhesive. It can be very helpful when working with tesserae that may be dislodged, and is very helpful for repairs. Most epoxies are waterproof.

• **MAC glue**: Available from mosaic specialty stores, MAC glue is a multipurpose, quick-drying, clear glue originally created by a glass artist for glass art. It is flexible, crystal clear, and water resistant, and rated as suitable for exterior use. Because it is thin it works best on flat and horizontal work surfaces, and a little goes a long way.

> **JARGON BUSTER**
> ◆ **MORTAR**
> *Mortar refers to a workable paste used as an adhesive or as grout.*

ADHESIVE	APPLICATIONS	SUGGESTED PROJECTS	WORK TIME	SKILL LEVEL	ADVANTAGES/ CHALLENGES
PVA glue (full strength)	Indoor Direct or mesh method	Artworks, any indoor project	20 mins		Easily available, safe, easy to clean up
PVA glue (diluted 50:50 with water)	Indoor and outdoor Indirect/reverse method	Table tops, floor medallions	1 hr		Easily available, safe, easy to clean up
Thinset	Indoor and outdoor Direct, double direct or indirect methods	Any permanent installation, inconsistent or heavy tesserae, submersion applications	30 mins		Easily available, convenient, must check manufacturer for exterior rating
Silicone adhesive	Outdoor Direct methods	Glass masonry, almost anything	10 mins		Easily available, some brands have a slight odor, sticky to work with
Mastic	Indoor Direct, double direct or indirect methods	Broken crockery and found objects	1 hr		Slight odor, very convenient
Epoxy glue	Outdoor Direct methods	Best for repairs	2 mins		Can be toxic, very sticky and very permanent
MAC glue	Indoor and outdoor Direct methods	Glass on glass	20 mins		Thin consistency, best used on flat surfaces

29
Gluing dos & dont's

Do

● Check, before buying, that the adhesive you have in mind is suitable to be used on your chosen substrate and for your final display.

● Follow the manufacturer's instructions and read the relevant health and safety information for any adhesive product you use.

● Work in a well-ventilated space.

● Wear rubber gloves when mixing and using thinset.

Don't

● Apply too much adhesive when laying mosaic tiles. Find the appropriate balance so that your tesserae achieve full adhesion without your grout lines becoming obscured.

● Pour unused cement-based adhesive down the sink or household drains.

● Forget to clean up any unused adhesive you have applied to your substrate when stopping work for the day.

FIX IT

30 Work neatly
It is important that the adhesive does not come up higher than the sides of the tesserae. Use a toothpick, flat-head screwdriver, or dental tool to help you tidy up the spaces in between each tile to make room for the grout.

Don't allow the thinset to come up higher than the sides of the tesserae.

Tidy up the spaces in between the tesserae to make room for the grout.

31
How much adhesive?

As a rule of thumb, regardless of your choice of tesserae and glue, the adhesive should cover 25 percent up the side of each tessera. This is easy to judge when using ceramic (as shown here), and a little trickier when using stained glass.

TRY IT

32 Wooden skewers
Use wooden skewers to help you push small pieces of tesserae into position. They are cheap, readily available, and disposable, and they will be far more accurate than your fingers alone. They are also helpful for cleaning your grout line in preparation for grouting.

33
Seating your tesserae

When working in the direct method with either PVA glue or thinset, it is best practice to properly "seat" each tessera. After applying adhesive, place the tessera in position, press, and twist. This "wiggle" will help the adhesive and tessera achieve a full "seat."

JARGON BUSTER ◆ BACK BUTTERING
Applying adhesive to the back of tesserae pieces.

Mixing thinset

Thinset is most commonly bought in powder form and mixed manually for small batches or with a paddle in a bucket for bigger jobs. Although thinset and grout are different—thinset is an adhesive, grout is not—they are both cement based and mixed in the same way. For instructions on how to mix thinset, see How to mix cement-based products, page 29.

Pre-mixed thinset

Thinset is available in a premixed form, and is stocked by most home improvement centers, which is great for small projects. Open the pail, use what you need, and reseal.

What size notched trowel should I use?

If you are working a large, flat area, it will be easiest to apply your thinset with a notched trowel. The size of the notches determines the amount of setting material that is put on the substrate. The notch size is determined by the size of the tile you are setting. The right notch size will give 100 percent coverage of thinset or mastic under the tesserae and allow the edge of the tesserae to be covered approximately 25 percent (see How much adhesive?, page 24). Most home stores selling thinset display a chart with the trowels detailing which size notch to use for the various thicknesses of tiles. You can also do a test coat to be sure the trowel size works with your tessarae size.

Coloring thinset

Thinset comes in two colors: white or gray. If your grout color is to be other than white or gray, you may want to color thinset using powdered paint pigment to approximately match the grout color. The thinset color may leach into your grout if it has not fully cured.

JARGON BUSTER ◆ ADMIX
Admix is a concentrated acrylic mortar additive. It increases the tensile and bond strength, water-resistance, and flexibility of thinset mortar and Portland cement grouts. As always, read the manufacturer's recommendations to determine its suitability for your project.

Gluing technique: thinset and mastic

Thinset and mastic are applied to the substrate using a notched trowel or palette knife.

1 I When a project requires you to apply the adhesive to a large part of the substrate, do so using a notched trowel. Flatten the trowel slightly to lay the adhesive down, but use it at a 90-degree angle to remove any excess. Make sure the teeth of the trowel touch the substrate to ensure an even thickness of adhesive is laid across the whole surface.

2 I Thinset or tile mastic are good choices when working directly onto a vertical or three-dimensional surface. The adhesive needs to be stiff, since if it is too wet the tiles may slip. In this case, an admix has been combined with thinset in a 50:50 ratio with water to give extra grip. Use a palette knife to apply small amounts of adhesive to the surface.

3 I Lay the tiles directly into the adhesive, giving each one a "wiggle" to properly seat it (see Seating your tesserae, page 24).

TRY IT

Just like decorating a cake
When working on smaller art projects, place thinset in a sandwich-size plastic bag, cut off a corner, and "squirt" the thinset exactly where you need it, much like decorating a cake with an icing bag. The bag also helps keep the adhesive moist for a longer working period.

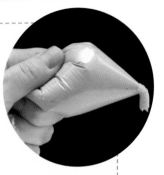

Gluing technique: PVA glue

PVA glue is an excellent choice when working directly (see pages 114–116), for which a good water-soluble variety is the best choice.

When working indirectly (see pages 124–129), a water-soluble PVA glue should be diluted with an equal amount of water to fix the tiles to the brown paper, which are then embedded in a cement-based adhesive. Whichever way of working, always precut your tiles and plan the area you are about to fix before applying any glue.

PVA glue becomes tacky and lumpy in five to ten minutes, so only apply glue to an area that you can tile in that time.

For direct working on areas of larger tiles, in uncomplicated patterns, you can apply PVA glue to the substrate with a spatula, paintbrush, or piece of firm cardstock, then place your tiles into the wet glue. Start cautiously, so that you don't lay down an area of glue larger than you can tile before the glue dries.

When working on detailed areas that require smaller pieces of tile, reverse your procedure: dab glue onto each piece of tile with a fine brush, then place it into the design. Try to work neatly to avoid getting glue on the surface of the tiles, although it can be removed later by peeling it off from the smooth surface of the tile.

Tweezers are very helpful if your mosaic work is small scale and detailed. Try holding your tesserae with the tweezers and dipping into a small amount of glue poured into an old plastic lid or surface you do not care about. Dip then place, give it a wiggle, and move on.

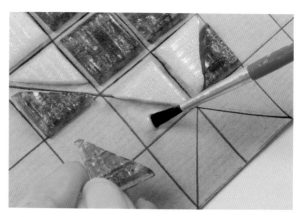

To fix tiles to brown paper for indirect working, dilute a water-soluble PVA glue with an equal amount of water and use a paintbrush to apply the glue to the paper or the tile. Flour paste, mucilage, or water-soluble school glue are also good choices for this technique.

Patience pays off

In order for PVA glue to set thoroughly, allow 24 hours between the time you finish gluing down a mosaic and grouting, otherwise the moisture in the grout may cause pieces to lift off.

FIX IT

42 **Dry glue too soon?**
If any area of PVA glue begins to set before you are ready to place tesserae, simply use a palette knife or hand spatula and smooth the glue so it dries smoothly and then reapply.

Wash the brush

When working with PVA glue you need to take care of your brush, since glue that has dried into the bristles cannot be removed, and the brush is rendered useless. At the end of a session, wash the brush in warm water with a mild detergent. If you have the opportunity to work over a whole day, you can wrap the brush tightly in plastic wrap when the time comes to take a break.

On the other hand, glue left to dry on a plastic spatula can simply be peeled off.

Decant PVA glue

To ensure you use PVA glue economically, transfer a small amount of glue to a disposable cup or other container and reseal the main container, to prevent the main stock of glue from drying out. When you take a break, tightly cover the glue in the container with plastic wrap to seal it. In this state the glue will remain usable for at least a day or two.

1 I Use a small amount of glue in a disposable container.

2 I Cover the cup with plastic wrap when you take a break to prevent it drying out.

Close the lid

Closing the lid on a bottle of glue whenever it is not in use will prevent spills and keep the nozzle clear.

FIX IT

46 **In from the cold**
Never allow your PVA glues to freeze, since this will break down the polymers and your glue will be rendered useless.

Grout: Choosing and using

The application of the grout that fills the gaps between the tesserae is the final act of creating the mosaic. The grout can transform the separate pieces of tesserae into a unified, coherent design. When you rub off the excess grout from the surface of the tiles, it is like seeing the design for the first time.

Choose your grout

Grout is available as sanded or unsanded, ready-mixed or in a powder form, and with or without latex additive. Almost all grouts from hardware and home stores are polymer fortified. Sanded grout is usually the most appropriate choice for mosaics, because grout lines are inconsistent, although many manufacturers recommend using unsanded grout for grout lines less than $^1/_{16}$in (2mm).

Colored grout

There is a generous range of ready-colored grouts available, from predictable whites, gray, and blacks to deep reds, purples, and blues. Colored grouts can be purchased from mosaic supply vendors or be specifically ordered from home centers or tile distributors. For information on coloring your own grout, see page 98.

Grouting dos & dont's

Do

● Follow the manufacturer's instructions and read the relevant health and safety information for any grout you use.

● Work in a well-ventilated space.

● Wear rubber gloves when mixing and using grout.

● For small projects, mix enough grout for your entire piece. For large projects, mix enough to work a manageable area.

● Store unmixed grout power in moisture-proof packaging. If the grout powder gets damp from humidity or is exposed to water, it will be rendered useless.

● Always wear a mask when mixing grout; grout contains silicate, which is dangerous to inhale.

● Have all of your grout tools handy: sponge, squeegee, paper towels or newsprint, tools for picking out grout from stubborn areas, and a buffing towel.

Don't

● Clean your grouting tools in the sink or pour water containing grout and cement-based adhesive down the drain. Cement can set even under water, so you will be endangering your plumbing and drainage systems if you do so.

● Don't be in a hurry; allow enough time to grout your project; once you begin the process you cannot leave it!

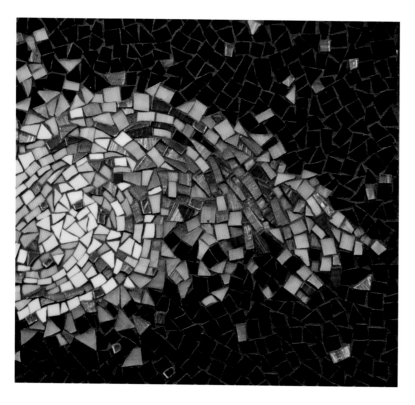

Left: Bonnie Fitzgerald used a dark grout to unify this piece, Spinning Nebula, *and to push the cosmic sky to the background, forcing the moving nebula to the forefront. The dark grout enhances the gold and copper tones and brings out the subtle blue of the stained glass and vitreous glass tesserae, adding dimension.*

Grouter's checklist

Take note of the following information with regards to mixing and using powdered thinset and grout, to ensure it is mixed properly, applied successfully, and used safely. These powders contain silica, lime, cement, and other materials that you must treat with caution.

• Wear gloves and a dust mask when working with powders.

• Once it has been mixed, thinset and grout must be set aside for a required amount of slaking time. Follow the manufacturer's recommendations. During slaking a chemical reaction is taking place, so it is important to be patient.

• Never add water or admix to grout or thinset after it has been slaked, because this will compromise the integrity of the mixture.

• Do not continue using a grout or thinset mixture after its stated period of working time.

• To help keep grout and thinset pliable and prevent a crust forming over it while you are working, stir frequently and lay a damp paper towel over the surface.

A helping hand

A good way to mix a large amount of thinset or grout is to use a power drill with a paddle attachment, the way it is done on construction sites.

How to mix cement-based products

Although thinset and grout are different—thinset is an adhesive, grout is not—they are both cement based and mixed in the same way. You should aim to mix up just enough to cover an area that you can use in one sitting. The product bag will give information on how much square footage the thinset or grout will cover.

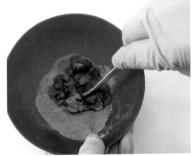

1 Wearing gloves and a dust mask, pour dry grout or thinset powder into a mixing container. Create a small well in the powder, and slowly add water. Use a palette knife or craft stick to stir together, adding small amounts of water at a time.

2 I Continue until the grout or thinset is smooth and has the consistency of stiff brownie batter. It is very easy to overwater your grout or thinset mixture. If you do overwater your mixture, try pouring some of the water off and then add more powder until you have your proper consistency. Some manufacturers do not recommend this. However, with a small art piece, where there is little wear and tear on the grout, it should be okay.

3 I If you think you need just a little more water, use a spray bottle to ensure you don't add too much.

When the correct consistency and volume has been reached, set aside to slake for the required time, following the manufacturer's directions.

54

Grouting technique

Whether you are using a ready-mixed grout or one you have mixed yourself, the method of applying it to the surface of the finished mosaic remains the same.

1 I A small mosaic can be grouted with your gloved hands or sponge; a large one will be better grouted with a grouting float or squeegee. Spread the grout in all directions, pushing the grout down into the spaces between the tiles. When the grout lines are completely filled in, use the side of your hand, the side of the float, or the squeegee to gently scrape the excess grout off the surface of the tiles. Remove as much grout as possible.

2 I Use a dry paper towel or a crumpled-up sheet of packing paper to carefully scrub the surface of the tiles to remove any leftover grout. It will be necessary to change paper as it gets messy until the tile surface is clean. Be careful not to dig into the grout lines and make divots in the grout. If this does happen, just take some grout and smear it into the damaged area, then wipe the surface smooth. Some artists use a damp sponge at this stage, but if too wet the sponge may pull out the grout.

> **JARGON BUSTER**
> **◆ CURE TIME**
>
> *As cement-based products, thinset and grout do not dry, they cure. The cure time refers to the time it takes for the chemical bond to activate and strengthen the silica and Portland cement, which can continue over 28 days.*

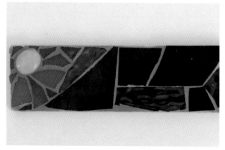

3 I Once the grout is pretty much cleaned off, set the mosaic aside for about 30 minutes to an hour, and allow the grout to start setting. You can use dental tools or dry paper towel to scrape off any stubborn grout that is still stuck to the face of the tiles.

4 I Take a clean paper towel or soft cloth and buff the face of the tiles to remove any haze. Repeat the buffing procedure the next day and double check to make sure that no grout remains where it shouldn't be. If it does, use your cleaning tools to remove it. If a tile falls out during grouting, carefully clean the area and repair later.

55

Quick cleanup

For safe and quick grouting cleanup, cover your work surface with newspaper or a disposable table cover before you begin. When you have finished working, gather up the paper with the grout mess inside and simply throw it all away.

FIX IT

56
Always reglue
Remember, grout has no adhesive qualities whatsoever. If you lose a tessera during the grouting process you must clean the area, reglue the tessera, and do a grout repair after the new adhesive has dried.

57
To seal or not to seal?

Grout is an extremely porous material that can harbor dirt, mold, mildew, and bacteria, which is why many artists choose to seal it. Over time grout may fade in color from direct sun, and many sealants provide UV protection. Sealing is always recommended for functional mosaics, such as shower inserts or tabletops, but for artworks and nonfunctional mosaics whether to seal or not is a personal choice.

If you do seal, use a professional-grade sealant, and do so at least 72 hours after the mosaic has been grouted. Most manufacturers recommend you also seal your grout periodically for the life of the installation.

58
Grouting is optional: direct set

Not all mosaics are grouted, instead they can be designed with the thinset or setting bed filling in the gaps between the tesserae. Working directly into the setting bed, the artist can see exactly what the final work will look like. The key to success is careful planning and patience.

Working in this way, you need to work methodically, applying just enough adhesive to a specific area, then moving on to the next. Some artists prefer to begin in the middle, others will begin at one corner or another, eventually mosaicking the entire "canvas."

Artists will often choose this method when working with smalti, marble and stone, found objects, and just about anything that grouting would detract from. The best adhesive choices for the direct set approach are thinset mortar or tile mastic, both of which can be colored with pigments.

Above: This work, Il Pavone by Jessica Maxson, is an excellent example of direct setting. The artist created the peacock by methodically working from the center outward, using smalti and marble in thinset.

JARGON BUSTER ♦ DIRECT SET

Artists working in the "direct set" method set their tesserae into a setting bed of mortar and do not grout. This is most common when working with smalti and found object tesserae.

2

All about tesserae

Tesserae are the building blocks of your mosaic, and the following chapter looks not only at the choices of material, but also at how to cut and lay these mosaic elements to create beautiful, striking, and intricate designs.

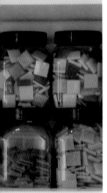

Know your tesserae

The term "tesserae," from the Latin word for cubes, originally referred to the square or cubed pieces of stone used in ancient, classical mosaics. Today, however, the word describes any pieces of mosaic material, from the commonly used vitreous glass, stained glass, and ceramic mosaic tiles to marble and found objects such as pebbles and shells. Each material has different properties that will affect how you use it and what your design will look like. The important thing about mosaic-making is not to see these properties as limitations, but to follow what the medium offers and to allow the materials to inspire you in ways you may not otherwise have considered.

 59

Vitreous glass and ceramic tesserae

Probably the most familiar tesserae are the vitreous glass and ceramic tiles that are manufactured as standard-size squares. Vitreous glass tiles are ideal for the novice mosaicist since they are easy to cut and are of a uniform thickness, resulting in mosaics that have a flat surface.

Ceramic tessarae can be split into two groups: porcelain and non-porcelain tiles. Porcelain tiles are frost resistant and available in unglazed, matte, and highly polished finishes. "Ceramic" or non-porcelain tiles are suitable for light-wear or decorative purposes and are almost always finished with a durable glaze which carries the color and pattern.

 60

Marble

Marble is a traditional mosaic material with natural color variations, available as rods or precut tesserae. It is thick and heavy, making it slightly tricky to fix in place. Marble can be honed by grinding to a fairly high polish. This brings out the color of the stone but produces a matte rather than a reflective surface, giving the marble a more natural appearance. Riven marble has been broken open to reveal its crystalline inner body, giving an interesting textured quality. Marble can also be polished, revealing its body color through a glossy finish.

61

Special sparkle

Gold smalti are sumptuous tesserae that consist of gold or white gold between two layers of glass: one thick to provide a strong base, and one very thin to protect the gold on top. Some have a textured, rippling effect. Also available are vitreous glass tiles backed with gold or silver leaf. Gold tiles can add a special magic and sparkle to your mosaic work, and although both of these types of tile are very costly, a little goes a long way. Try cutting very small pieces and using them sparingly in the piece; the light will reflect off the gold or silver metallic finish in unexpected ways, transforming an otherwise dull mosaic into a glistening work of art.

Above: Gold tesserae look great even used sparingly.

TRY IT

62 **Cheap trick**
Including mirror is a great way to add "bling" to your mosaic, and is super inexpensive. Mirror is simply silver painted on the back of glass. To keep the mirror from degrading over time (it will react with the glue) you must "seal" the mirror with mirror sealant, readily available anywhere that sells glass.

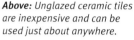

Above: Unglazed ceramic tiles are inexpensive and can be used just about anywhere.

Above: Vitreous glass tiles have two sides. The top—the side you will see—is smooth; the underside is textured to help the adhesive grip the tile.

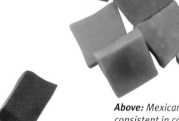

Above: Glazed ceramic tiles come in a huge variety of sizes and glaze finishes. Be sure to check they are weather resistant if you plan to use them outside.

Above: Polished marble cubes can be purchased loose or in sheet form. When it is in sheets, it is often stuck to the mesh with waterproof glue, so it is safer to buy a mix of marble cubes than to risk being unable to soak the marble off the mesh.

Above: Italian smalti is very consistent in color and size. The "inside" or "riven" edge of the slab is the most beautiful piece of the glass and the most often used.

TRY IT

63 **Sourcing marble offcuts**
You can cut your own marble rods on a wet saw with the appropriate saw blade. Often home stores or tile distributors have broken pieces or a few leftover pieces from an installation that they are happy give away.

Above: Mexican smalti is not consistent in color and size varies. Each side of the slab is different, so the artist can use front, back, or inside, since all sides have their own unique beauty.

65

Smalti

Smalti is handmade enamelized glass manufactured in Italy and Mexico. Smalti has been the material of choice of master mosaicists throughout the world for over a century. It has richness, reflectivity, and a depth of color that just cannot be matched. Smalti is made by pouring slabs of glass from which "pizzas" (in Italy), "tortillas" (in Mexico), rectangular (Italy) or square (Mexico) tesserae are cut. Smalti "B" cuts refer to uncut smalti pieces which can be cut with a hammer and hardie into any size, or be used in larger pieces as part of a mixed-media artwork.

Above: In order to create cubes, marble tiles are first cut into lengths known as rods, and purchasing the rods is cheaper than buying the precut cubes. These lengths of marble can be used as they are, offering a contrast of scale, or be cut into cubes (see Rods to cubes: open wide, page 44).

FIX IT

64 **Protect with sealant**
Polished marble gains some chemical resistance to staining from the structure of its glassy surface, but honed or riven marble is more vulnerable and needs protection. To give terracotta and marble some protection from dirt and grime, apply a sealant. If you are making a tabletop with marble tiles, it is a good idea to use a sealant that also protects it against staining from spillages of oil and wine.

Left: Millefiori can be mixed with other more conventional mosaic materials as details or highlights. They can also be used completely on their own, in which case you should experiment with the layout before gluing. If you plan to grout, pack the milleflori densely, otherwise they will be swamped by the grout.

66
Millefiori

Milleflori are small round or rectangular beads cut from glass rods and traditionally made on the island of Murano, Italy. Layers of glass in a mold are heated in a furnace then pulled until thin, while still maintaining the cross section's design. Once cooled, the rods are cut into beads or disks. Milleflori can bring intense color and interest to a project.

68
Stained glass

Stained glass is a popular and economical mosaic material, and we have the explosion of art glass and glass fusing to thank for providing mosaics artists with new and exciting stained-glass products to incorporate into their work. Stained glass has a vast color selection and many manufacturers are creating breathtaking glasswork. It is easy to use, economically priced, and easy to obtain.

Stained glass varies in opacity: it can be transparent—often referred to as cathedral—translucent, or opaque. It is available in textures of smooth, crinkled, seedy, or many other examples, and in surface finishes such as iridized or molted.

FIX IT
67 **Remedy a mixed-color background**
It can be very frustrating, and look rather strange, if the tesserae colors in a single-color background change slightly halfway across a piece (see Keep an eye on color, page 37). If this does happen, however, it can be remedied. Rather than soaking off all the mosaic and starting again, randomly peel off some tiles in the area you have already laid, and make a mixture of the old and the new color batches across the whole area, to give an interesting and flickery effect.

TRY IT
69 **Make your own tesserae**
Experiment by creating your own signature mosaic tesserae, using materials such as polymer clay, air-dry clay, papier mâché, and many more.

Above: This playful mosaic, Road Hog by Andrea Shreve Taylor, uses traditional materials, such as stained glass, as well as found objects to comic effect, and demonstrates how you can use almost anything in your mosaic work.

70
Improvised tesserae

Almost anything you can think of can be used as mosaic tesserae. Found objects—such as recycled crockery, beads and buttons, and natural materials including shells and pebbles—provide a rich source of alternatives for creating unconventional mosaic work.

71

Keep an eye on color

It is worth noting that batches of the same color tesserae from different suppliers—or even the same supplier—can feature color variations. If you are working on a large mosaic with one primary background color, make sure you purchase all the tiles you will need (see How to estimate quantities, below) from the same supplier and at the same time. If you run out of tiles halfway down and order a new batch of tesserae, you might find that the color of the new tiles is slightly different to that of the old ones (see Remedy a mixed-color background, page 36).

Tesserae colors can vary. Make sure you have ordered enough material from the same supplier before embarking on a mosaic with a solid single-color background.

TRY IT

72 **Testing materials for exterior applications**

The simplest way to determine feasibility of tesserae materials for year-round outdoor use is to check with the manufacturer. When that is not possible, use this simple technique for simulating dramatic weather changes. Wet a piece of the tesserae material and place it in a freezer overnight, then allow it to thaw the next day. Repeat the same process for a few more days. If the material cracks or breaks, it is obviously not suitable for year-round exterior application in a freeze/thaw environment.

73

How to estimate quantities

It is challenging to calculate the exact number of tiles a specific mosaic will require, since wastage will depend on your skill at cutting tiles and the complexity of the design. However, a good general guide is to calculate the approximate area you want to cover and add 15 percent for wastage. This is the minimum amount of tesserae you will need. Next, estimate the percentage of the different colors that make up your design.

Mosaic suppliers sell tesserae in a variety of ways: some by the pound, others by square footage, sometimes loose, sometimes mounted on sheets. The list at right gives examples of some standard quantities and the area these can be estimated to cover.

Keep track of how many tiles you use for each project and compare this to the number you ordered. This will allow you to more accurately predict the number of tiles that an individual project is likely to require in the future.

Material	How it is sold	Approximate coverage
Vitreous glass tiles (¾in, 2cm) square	Sheets or partial sheets	225 tiles = 1 sq. ft (30 sq. cm)
	Loose by weight	1lb (0.4kg) = 6 sq. ft (1.8 sq. m)
Unglazed ceramic/porcelain tiles (¾–1in, 2–2.5cm square)	Sheets or partial sheets	196–225 tiles = 1–1¼ sq. ft (30–40 sq. cm)
	Loose by weight	1lb (0.4kg) = 7½ sq. ft (2.3 sq. m)
Household ceramic tiles	Individually	Varies
	Case	Case = 9 sq. ft (2.7 sq. m)
Smalti	Loose by weight	2¾lb (1.25kg) = 1 sq. ft (30 sq. cm)
Stained glass	Sheet	Sheet = 1 sq. ft (30 sq. cm)

74

Economical sourcing

Vitreous glass and ceramic mosaic tiles can be bought loose from craft stores, often in bags featuring random or tonal mixes of colors, but these can be expensive. Mosaic supply companies can be found on the Internet (see also Resources, page 154) and they offer the best prices on small amounts of tile, especially if you are shopping for modest amounts of several colors.

An even more economical way to buy these tiles is as sheets of single or mixed colors, attached to a paper or mesh backing. The sheets are intended to hold the individual tiles in place so that they can be applied more easily and quickly when used for domestic tiling applications. To use these tiles in your own designs, simply soak the sheet in soapy warm water and pull the individual tiles off.

FIX IT

Making life easier

76 Be wary of buying sheets of glass or ceramic tesserae attached with blobs of rubberlike adhesive: you will have to snip them apart with scissors, which can be a real nuisance.

 75

Go compare

Your first consideration when choosing tesserae must be a practical one—make sure the tiles or improvised materials you choose are suitable for the conditions the mosaic is to exist in, for example, if the mosaic is to be sited outdoors, the tiles need to be frost-resistant. The following table provides an at-a-glance guide to the pros and cons of the various types of tesserae.

MATERIAL	APPLICATIONS	SIZE RANGE
1 **Stained glass**	Interior and exterior. Good for walls and art pieces. Not good for floors.	Any
2 **Vitreous glass**	Interior and exterior. Good for walls, ceilings, tables, and decorative objects. Not good for floors.	¼in–1in (0.5–2.5cm) squares
3 **Unglazed ceramic/ porcelain**	Interior and exterior. Hard-wearing and particularly suitable for use on floors.	Range in size, depending on manufacturer, ¾–1in (2–2.5cm) squares
4 **Glazed ceramic**	Check with manufacturer, some tiles may not be frost-resistant. Not suitable for floors.	Variety of sizes and shapes
5 **Marble**	Interior and exterior.	Various
6 **Smalti**	Interior and exterior. Smalti's fractured face and pitted body make it unsuitable for floors.	Sizes vary, but in the region of ⅓in (8mm) thick x ⅔in (15mm) long
7 **Millefiori**	Interior and exterior.	Various
8 **Household ceramic tiles**	Interior. The wall tiles are brittle and slippery so not suitable for floors.	Various, 1–12in (2.5–30cm) squares and rectangles
9 **Found objects**	Various. Pebbles and stones are particularly suited to outdoor applications, since they are already weatherproof.	Various

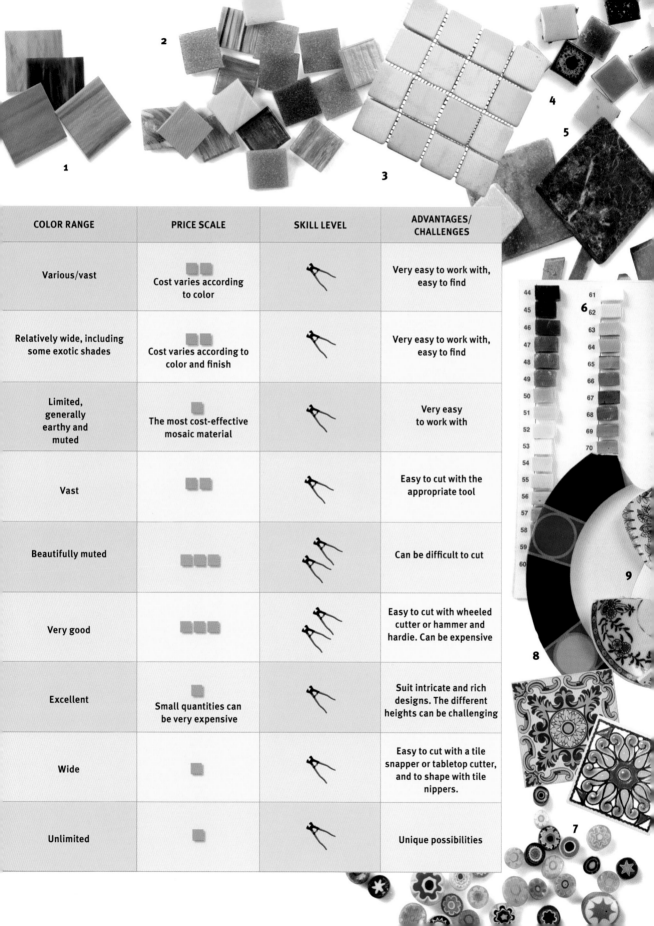

COLOR RANGE	PRICE SCALE	SKILL LEVEL	ADVANTAGES/CHALLENGES
Various/vast	Cost varies according to color		Very easy to work with, easy to find
Relatively wide, including some exotic shades	Cost varies according to color and finish		Very easy to work with, easy to find
Limited, generally earthy and muted	The most cost-effective mosaic material		Very easy to work with
Vast			Easy to cut with the appropriate tool
Beautifully muted			Can be difficult to cut
Very good			Easy to cut with wheeled cutter or hammer and hardie. Can be expensive
Excellent	Small quantities can be very expensive		Suit intricate and rich designs. The different heights can be challenging
Wide			Easy to cut with a tile snapper or tabletop cutter, and to shape with tile nippers.
Unlimited			Unique possibilities

Choosing tesserae project: Millefiori heart

This project uses vitreous glass tiles, gold-backed glass tiles, and millefiori to illustrate the wonderful effects that can be achieved by mixing your tesserae. The order in which you tackle the piece is very important. Key "outlines" are tiled first to provide a container, which is then filled in with other tiles. This is a good technique to adopt when tackling many other designs too—it ensures your fills don't wander and blur the patteren.

6¹/₂in (16.5cm)

6¹/₂in (16.5cm)

▲ *To scale and transfer the design, follow the techniques described on pages 78–79. This project has been photographed working on a white substrate and without using glue, to more clearly illustrate the techniques described.*

Palette

Bright orange *Dark red*

Rose *Yellow*

You will need

Vitreous glass tesserae

Gold-leaf tesserae

Millefiori

Paper for transferring the design

Pen or grease pencil to mark the tiles

Wheel cutters or tile nippers

Adhesive and gluing tools

Grout and grouting tools

▲ **1** | Start by filling in the shape of the heart with the millefiori. Use tiles of different diameters and pack them in such a way as to increase the density of tiles and minimize the gaps in between that will hold the grout.

▲ **2** | Outline the heart with small gold-leaf tiles. Surround the heart with half-moon tiles—the deep red picks up the predominant color in the millefiori, while providing a dark outline to the central motif. You'll notice in this example that all "warm" colors have been used—red, rose, and yellow—which add to the rich intensity of the piece.

▶ **3** | Place teardrop-cut tiles between the half-moons to add a final outline effect to the central motif, using a lighter, but still bright, color— here, orange.

▶ **4** | Next, fill in the square that surrounds the central heart, using a checkerboard-type fill, done here with quarters of whole glass tiles that have then been split in half again to make tiny rectangles.

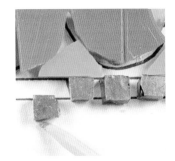

◀ 5 | The semicircular motifs that surround the checkerboard are made up of two symmetrical halves, made by splitting a tile diagonally then shaping the cut edge to fashion it into a quarter-moon shape.

▲ 6 | Fill the shape between the semicircles with simple triangles, before outlining the square with more of the tiny gold tiles.

◀ 7 | Place a whole tile at the four corners to establish the line of the outer border. Now go back to your millefiori tiles and select similarly sized pieces of tile to create the triangles of the outer border. Finally, use more triangular cuts of whole tiles, matching the ones placed in the corners, to fill the space between the millefiori triangles.

▶ This project can be completed by gluing and grouting using the direct method (see pages 114–116). The finished piece will have an uneven surface because of the mixture of tiles used, so the final grouting is quite tricky. You may need to excavate smaller tiles that get submerged by the grout by scraping away excess grout with a wooden skewer.

 77

Embrace imperfection

Most vitreous glass tiles are manufactured with a beveled edge along all four sides of the tile. When you cut small, intricate shapes, the bevel will sometimes mean the tessera is stuck at a slight angle. Embrace this. It is these slightly different surface imperfections that allow the light to reflect in unexpected and beautiful ways.

Cutting with confidence

A good cutting technique will allow you to create tesserae to fit your design and ensure that you make the most of different materials. It does take a little practice, and even when you are experienced some materials just won't cut how you want them to. Thankfully, for many designs, you do not need to worry about absolute precision when cutting. Mosaics are very forgiving. When you look at an image made in mosaic, particularly one that depends on color, you tend to focus on the entire image, rather than the cutting.

FIX IT

78 Stand up
Always stand when you are first learning to cut stained glass, since you will more easily be able to control the score and see exactly what you are doing. You can get better pressure from your shoulder than your wrist.

79
Look to the smooth

When cutting stained glass, always score the glass on its smoothest side.

80
Warm it up

Glass does not like being cut when it is cold. If the glass is cold to the touch, run it under warm (not hot!) water before cutting.

FIX IT

81 Dip it
If your glass cutter is not self-lubricating, dip it in glass cutter oil periodically between scores.

82
Preparing stained glass for mosaic

The most common way to purchase stained glass is in sheets—often called "hobby sheets"—that measure approximately 12 x 12in (30 x 30cm). To cut shapes from the sheets you will need three tools: an oil-carbide glass cutter to score the glass, a runner to "run" the score, and a wheel cutter to cut smaller shapes. A good-quality oil-carbide glass cutter is not very expensive. It is a necessary investment if you regularly use stained glass in your mosaics. The most popular for the hobby crafter are the pencil-grip cutters or fist-grip cutters. Either works fine, and the final choice comes down personal preferences.

1 I Hold the glass securely with one hand while scoring with the other. Begin to cut ⅟₁₆in (2mm) from the edge of the glass, running a score from edge to edge of the glass.

2 I Maintain an even pressure while scoring. Your score line should be visible, and a gentle ripping sound heard. Never go over the same score line, because the glass will not properly break.

3 I Use the runner to "run" the score, which actually breaks the glass.

83

Using wheel cutters

Wheel cutters are the tool most commonly used by mosaic artists working in glass. There are many cutters on the market, and you should purchase the very best you can afford, since the better the tool the more life you will have with it. For information on cutting shapes, see pages 46–47.

1 I An efficient way to cut stained glass into smaller tessarae is to first cut the sheet glass into strips. If you want consistent, same-size pieces, use a straight edge. If you prefer a more organic feel, cut the strips freehand.

2 I To cut vitreous glass or stained-glass tesserae, make sure the wheel is perpendicular to the glass at all times. The wheels should face your stomach, regardless of whether you are right or left handed. Place the wheels where the desired cut is to be and cut quickly. Moving too slowly as you squeeze the wheel tool can shatter the glass.

 84

Using tile nippers

Tile nippers are used to cut vitreous glass tesserae and ceramic. The idea is to create a fault line that the tile splits along—a line that is a continuation of the nipper blades.

1 I Hold the nippers in your main hand with the cutting edges facing your other hand. Grasp the handles near the ends for optimum cutting strength.

2 I To cut a tile into halves or quarters, place ⅙–¼in (4–6mm) of the edge of the tessera into the jaws of the nippers at 90 degrees to them. Gently squeeze the handles to make the cut—the tile will split along the line of the blades of the nipper. To cut more precise shapes you will need to the use the tile nippers' ability to "nibble" (see page 47).

 85

Cut across the grain

Some vitreous glass tesserae have a slight grain in them, and will cut more reliably across the grain than along it.

 86

Using tile snappers

Tile snappers have a scoring wheel and snapping mechanism, and can be used to make accurate straight cuts in vitreous glass and ceramic tesserae.

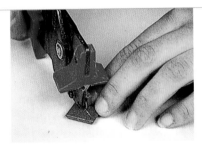

1 I Score the tile from corner to corner, pressing hard. If you do not get a good score the first time round, move your score line slightly to one side—you cannot score in the same place as it is likely you will shatter your tile.

2 I Next, place the mosaic tile so the score line runs along the shaft of the snapping mechanism. Press gently but firmly—don't be too timid, since you may crumble the corners off the tile.

87

Cutting unglazed ceramic

Unglazed ceramic tesserae have a very flat face and an unreflective surface, so you notice the effect of the cuts you make more than with any other material. You can use this to your advantage in your designs.

88

Marble: a different approach

The veining and stresses that occur naturally within marble mean that it may crumble or fracture if you try to cut with nippers from the edge. Instead, place the nippers centrally along the line you wish to break and exert sharp pressure. If you try to cut too slowly, this can make the material crumble, and sorting out badly formed cuts is trickier with this material than with any other, not least because of its thickness.

When cutting down precut marble cubes, place the whole cube within the jaws of the tile nippers.

89

Rods to cubes: open wide

Marble rods are less expensive than precut cubes, and can be cut with tile nippers. If the nippers will not open wide enough to take the depth of the marble, remove the spring, which is not essential for the nippers to function.

Cutting cubes from marble rods is more economical than buying them precut.

90

Try traditional

The traditional way of cutting stone tesserae, using a hammer and hardie, is particularly suited to cutting marble. The hammer ends with a pointed blade and is used in conjunction with a chisel-type blade, stuck in a log, which is known as a hardie. To cut, place your tile over the hardie so the blade expresses the direction you want the break to go in. Do not swing the hammer, but let it fall with its own weight onto the marble. The process is not as hazardous as it looks, although the occasional blood blister is probably inevitable.

1 I Hold the marble cube over the hardie blade at the angle at which you want it to break.

2 I Bring the hammer down to crack the cube. If you cut too heavily, the two blades will meet and blunt one another.

91

Cutting household ceramic tiles down to size

Just like ceramic and vitreous glass tesserae, household ceramic tiles can be cut into mosaic elements using tile nippers. However, it is a good idea to break the large tile down into manageable-sized strips first.

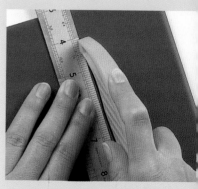

1 I To do this by hand, use a tile scorer and tile snapper. Score the glazed surface in a straight line along the width of the tile, using a metal ruler to guide you. Apply pressure with the scorer, taking care not to let it slip across the tile.

TRY IT

92 Make your own riven marble

Riven marble is created by a cutting process that you can replicate for yourself. Place a marble cube within the jaws of your tile nippers and exert sharp pressure. By cutting it in half, you create a rectangular rather than a square piece and reveal the crystalline inner body of the stone, which becomes your top surface. Continue nipping down until you reach the desired shape.

Riven marble has a textured face.

2 I Slowly and firmly squeeze the handles of the tile snapper to break the tile cleanly along the score line.

3 I Repeat the same process to make a number of strips of tile of equal widths. These strips can now be easily cut into square tiles using tile nippers in the usual way.

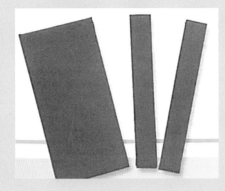

4 I A tabletop tile cutter, sometimes called a snap and rail cutter, can also be used to cut larger format ceramic tiles—this is probably the easiest and least expensive tool. Place the tile on the cutter and drag the scoring wheel across the tile. Then press the foot of the heel assembly against the tile to snap the scored pieces apart.

Using your tile nipper, cut the broken pieces into smaller tesserae, working to isolate the decorative elements you specifically wish to incorporate into your mosaic. Here, pieces of a decorative tile provide a patterned infill to sections of a frame.

93

Get smashing

The best way of breaking a plate or saucer down to a manageable size for cutting with tile nippers is to place it inside a plastic bag—to contain the fragments—then strike it firmly in the center with a hammer. When it comes to honing in on the required motif with the nippers, be aware that old china can be difficult to work with and can break unpredictably. It can also sometimes cut you unexpectedly, so use caution.

1 I Once the piece is inside the bag, secure the top with an elastic band or tuck it underneath, then hit the plate with the hammer.

2 I Use tile nippers to work on the fragments and to take off the excess tile from around the motif or section of pattern you want to use. Carefully nibble at the crockery piece to achieve the desired shape.

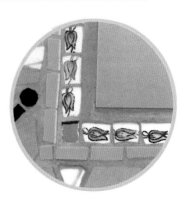

Here, patterned fragments from an old plate provide an interesting border detail.

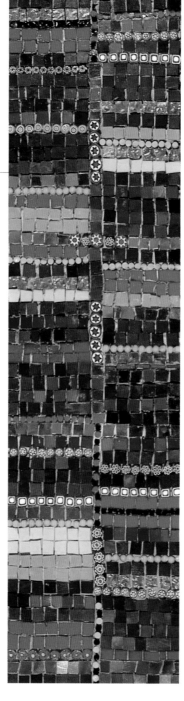

94

Half and half again

You can cut standard vitreous glass tiles and ceramic mosaic tiles in half and in half again—making quarter-tiles—and so on, until the preferred size is achieved. A quarter of a standard mosaic tile makes a good base unit to work with, not too big and not too small. Half-units will cover the ground more quickly, but are directional. Eighths, sixteenths, and smaller are versatile but quite fiddly.

Right: Using only the simplest of cuts can provide the mosaicist with endless variation. This eye-catching quilt detail, by Bonnie Fitzgerald, is made up of half, whole, quartered tiles, and millefiori.

95

Cutting triangles

Triangles are a staple shape of mosaics, but they can be challenging to cut, and you can expect lots of waste.

1 I Mark a diagonal line from corner to corner across the top side of the tesserae—the beveled edge should not be visible.

2 I Hold the tesserae between thumb and first finger, without obscuring the line. Take the wheel cutters in your other hand and place the wheels on the line. Squeeze the handles of the cutters with a confident pressure, and don't snatch or try to twist the tile.

FIX IT

96 **Ouch, I have a tiny, pointed shard of glass in my finger!**
Place a small piece of very sticky tape over the area and use it to pull the glass out.

FIX IT

97 **Keep calm and carry on**
Try not to get frustrated at the number of times a cut goes wrong. Even the most experienced mosaicist will tell you that for every "good" shape they cut, three or four shapes invariably end up in the trash can. Glass tiles in particular are highly unpredictable. No matter how accurately you follow the cut line with the your cutting tool, the tile still may not cut cleanly and evenly. However, you can sometimes rescue "bad" cuts by nibbling back to the original line.

98
Nibble

When it comes to cutting specific shapes, you will need to "nibble."

Wheel cutters have beveled blades that allow you to nibble the corners off tesserae to make circles or other special shapes.

You can also nibble with the tile nipper, which has sharp beveled edges.

Nibble the edge of the tile away to create your chosen shape.

99
Useful cutting sequences

Small circles
To cut a half-size circle, cut the tile in half along the diagonal, then nibble out the shape as usual.

Small triangles
You can halve this tile once again to make an even smaller triangle.

Half-moons
To create a half-moon, first split the tile in half. Starting from one corner, nibble around the drawn curve.

Crescents
Cut the outer curve of the crescent, then grip the tile firmly between thumb and forefinger and cut a very little at a time along the inner curve with the very edge of the nippers, otherwise you may shatter the tile.

100
Cutting circles

Cutting circular shapes requires lots of individual cuts and is physically strenuous work. The best way to avoid shattering is to only nibble a little at a time. Begin with a piece of glass just a bit larger than the circle size you desire and methodically nibble your way around.

1 | Begin by carefully drawing the circle on the top side of your chosen tile—you will find it very difficult to cut a circle by eye.

2 | Place the cutting tool on the tile opposite your hand and cut inward to the line of the circle. Rotate the tile counterclockwise by a few degrees, then cut inward again from the edge of the tile to continue the curve of the circle. Repeat until you have rotated the tile through a complete circle.

TRY IT

101 Use a template
An easier alternative to drawing freehand circles—especially if you need to cut many circles—is to find a circular shape to use as an outline. Try coins, buttons, washers, bottletops, or an artist's circle template.

Templates: Beasts, birds, and bugs

In mosaic art, animals make beautiful, funny, charming, compelling, and moving subjects. Birds come in many shapes and sizes, and have proved a powerful inspiration to mosaicists. While insects make fascinating motifs for mosaic, maybe because capturing the contrast between delicate wings and firmly defined legs and bodies is a rewarding challenge.

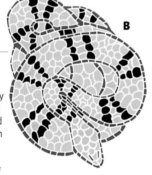

102

Coiled snake ▶

This beautiful snake is coiled very realistically. The strong outline is necessary to define the coils, and is also decorative. Note how each tessera on the snake's body has been roughly rounded to imitate the snakeskin pattern—the motif is composed simply of dots and curving lines—and the bars across the snake's body are worked in a dark, light, and midtone. The variation is poisonously bright.

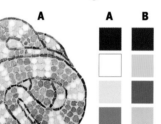

103

Goat ▶

A mosaic goat is depicted with strength and vitality, which suits a creature associated with agility and abundant energy. The hide of the goat is broken up into areas of bold color to imitate its shaggy coat and muscular form. These areas are full of curves and movement. The horns have had the same confident treatment applied to decorative effect. This motif does not have to be treated in a naturalistic way, as is illustrated in the more playful approach of the alternative colorway.

104

Ginger cat ▲

Tail up, this ginger cat stands with its green eye calmly gazing ahead. The use of slightly varying brown tones on the body gives a gently rounded effect. The shadowy undercarriage, made from darker tesserae, emphasizes light falling from above. Spotty and stripy variations are also possible, using natural shades or completely unnatural colors, just for fun.

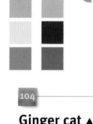

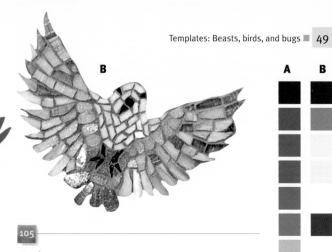

105
Owl ▲

A flying owl displays a wonderful sweep of wings, its feathers braced against the air current. Every feather has been individually constructed; the pointed ends create a dramatic jagged outline. Touches of bronze metallic smalti amid the ghostly whites and grays add to the magic. The variation combines cold greens with closely related "warm" blues, with a strong, "warm" green for the flashes on the wings.

108
Pet portrait

Consider making a portrait of your own pet. Create a cartoon pattern from a photograph and immortalize your furry friend.

106
Terrier ▶

This pebble mosaic, depicting a real terrier called Dorothy, illustrates her marvelously sturdy character. If you cannot find pebbles in the different tones suggested for the variation, you could shape tesserae instead to gain a similar effect, although it may not be a quick option. Note in each case how the judicious use of a few lines of black pebbles helps to define the dog's form.

107
Seated hare ▶

Much of the success of this hare mosaic is due to its dynamic outline. The molding is beautifully thought out, the lighter areas tending to avoid the outline, leaving it strong and dark, all except for the tender, vulnerable, soft underbelly. The original uses fairly natural shades, so a more colorful variation is suggested, one that remains true to the tonal composition.

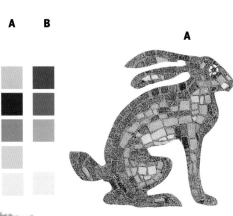

A B

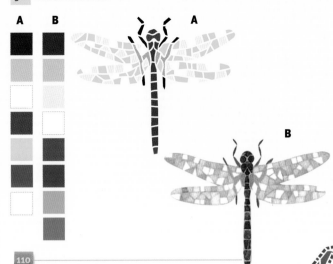

A

B

Aztec lizard ▼

The zigzag lines and diamond patterns on the lizard's back give this mosaic a Mexican feel. It utilizes plenty of bright colors, similar in tone, which are fairly evenly dispersed about the motif. The black outline tesserae hold it all together. A similarly bright alternative could be tried, remembering to always use a dark tone to outline the overall shape.

A

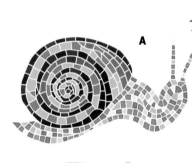

B

A B

110

Classic dragonfly ▲

Beautifully balanced tonally, this classic dragonfly mosaic depicts light, fluttery wings, by using pale and varied tesserae, and a darker body and head in more solid colors. Note how the legs are more shadowy when seen through the wings. A mix of bright hues on the variation creates a fun alternative.

A B

A

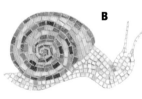

B

A B

112

Multicolored snail ▲

Snails provide the perfect opportunity to employ a popular mosaic pattern—the spiral. Starting from the center with a light and a dark line, and winding outward, extra lines are introduced and removed as the coils of the shell grow wider. Long tesserae are used in the shell to emphasize the linear effect. The shell colors are all warm shades, although they vary tonally from deep brown-black to pale yellow. The snail's body has less contrast, mingling pale shades of pink. The variation mixes several colors for the shell and the body.

111

Hen ▼

Many of the tesserae have been individually cut into lozenge shapes to form this cheerful hen mosaic, and the grout plays a prominent part in showing them up. The eye looks as though it has been painted on; another way of achieving this effect is to drill a shallow indentation into the tessera after it has been grouted and has set, then rub a little grout of your chosen color into the indentation. A greater tonal mix has been used in the variation, although the color scheme is similar.

A

B

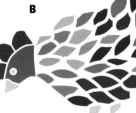

A B

113

Butterfly ▶

The wings of this butterfly feature several graded shades of soft blue that create a sense of delicacy, but the black dots and triangles prevent the mosaic from being too fragile. The variation changes the blues for pinks.

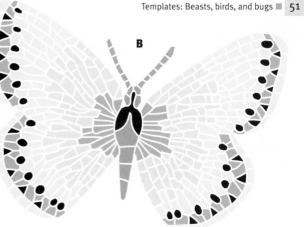

B

A

114

Ram ▼

A little like a Roualt painting, this ram mosaic makes great use of its black outline to give it a fierce strength. Unless one is embarking on some very subtle foreshortening, areas such as the ram's head need this kind of definite treatment to tell the onlooker what is happening; in this case, that the head and horn are in front of, and more important than, the shoulder. The variation maintains the tonal formula, but uses more impressionistic hues.

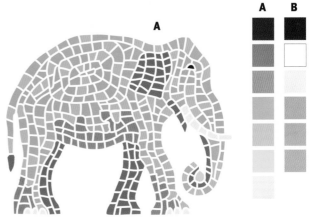

A

A B

A

115

Elephant ▲

Elephants are associated with wisdom, patience, and longevity; all qualities the mosaicist may like to meditate on when at work. This charming mosaic is not complicated, but flows in a pleasing and logical manner by following the form of the elephant in a most natural way. At the furthest extreme from the gentle grays of the original is a color variation inspired by the vivid hues of Indian embroidery.

B

A B

B

116

Try a representational mosaic

Creating a mosaic animal is a great way to begin your journey into representational mosaic art. They do not need to be reproduced perfectly or in the exact colors of the subject and they lend themselves to stylized, graphic interpretations.

About andamento

The most fundamental decisions you will make when designing your mosaic concern the andamento. This term refers to the way the tesserae flow, the system you select to carry out each area of your design; it is the mosaic equivalent of the brushstroke. The physical flow of the tiles—whether a smooth contouring around the design, or a jagged fill that agitates the piece—helps to give form to the mosaic and create mood and effect.

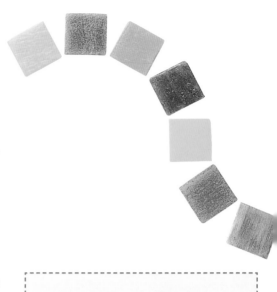

> **JARGON BUSTER • ANDAMENTO**
> *The word used to describe the flow or direction of the mosaic, determined by the placement of the tesserae and the grout lines.*

117
Know your classical opus

Some traditional and often-used andamento techniques have their own categorizations, each with its own "opus" name—Latin for "work." The second part of each opus name describes the style of laying, also based on Latin terminology. These terms are shorthand ways of describing the system by which the tiles in any mosaic are laid relative to one another. Once you begin to take notice of the different types of opus you will appreciate how varied their effects on a mosaic's final appearance can be.

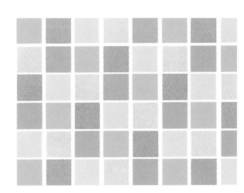

118
Opus regulatum

The tesserae is laid out in a regular grid, both horizontally and vertically. The appeal of mosaic laid in this way is that it is calming as a background. If the main features of your mosaic are lively and frantic, or the colors particularly bright, this background might be a good choice as a contrast.

Right: This mosaic contrasts the leaping vitality of the dog with an ordered geometric background of opus regulatum, a contradiction of stillness and movement.

Above: *The starfish has wonderful impact in both color and form, which is accentuated by the calming effect of the opus tesellatum background.*

119

Opus tessellatum

The tesserae form rows in one direction—either horizontally or vertically—but in the other direction the tesserae are staggered informally. It is important that the tesserae don't match up across the rows, since this will detract from the harmony. Like opus regulatum, this opus lends a sense of stillness and solidity to a design.

120

Opus palladianum

The "crazy paving" opus, where irregular tesserae fit together, the only rule being that the gaps between the tiles are approximately the same width. It makes a lively, directionless pattern that adds a sizzle to a mosaic, although if used excessively, it can be a little tiring to look at.

Right: *The effect of this opus is lively and free.*

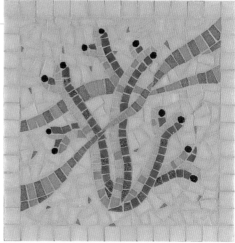

121

Opus circumactum

Related to the traditional mosaic fan shape (see Designing a repeat fan tessellation, page 104), opus circumactum is useful for square mosaics, where the tiles are laid in quarter-circles from the edge, and meet neatly in the center. The effect is rhythmic, undulating, and gives a sense of movement without being overbearing.

Left: *Opus circumactum is ideal for this panel, because it gives the impression of waves or ripples, which complements the subject, as well as providing a lively—but not too distracting—background.*

122

Opus vermiculatum

An outlining technique that gives a shape its own energy and space. A row—or several rows—of tesserae carefully follows a shape, emphasizing its outline. Used on a large scale it can have a wonderful effect. You can use it to give a hierarchy to images by surrounding the most significant motifs with the widest flowing lines.

Right: *Bonnie Fitzgerald's* Potomac River Fish *uses opus vermiculatum to subtly make the vitreous glass fish stand out from their neutral background.*

123

Opus musivum

A continuation of opus vermiculatum, where the tesserae continue to flow outward following the contours of the outline, filling the entire background. This dynamic opus creates a sense flow and movement, and can bring a mosaic to life.

Above: *In this reproduction of* Zippori, *artist George Fishman captures flow and movement around the main subject by outlining and following the contours. This style of opus was used widely in early Byzantine mosaics.*

124

Opus sectile

Sitting at the boundaries of true mosaic, and close to traditional stained glass territory, each tessera is cut to form a complete shape in itself.

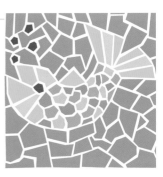

Above: *Andrea Shreve Taylor uses opus sectile in her mosaic,* Sammy, *to create a visually lively artwork. The large pieces of stained glass in the foreground neatly fit together in a traditional stained-glass manner. The millefiori add texture and interest.*

TRY IT

125 **Mix it up**

You only need to look at a handful of mosaics to know that artists rarely use just one type of opus in a single mosaic. Try different mixes of opus on the same design to discover how each combination of treatments affects the feel of the finished piece. The examples here show how you can mix different opus in different parts of your design to give a distinct effect.

Right: The opposite of the first example, here the central shape is filled with opus musivum, while the background is opus regulatum, resulting in a more contemporary feel. This combination flattens and neutralizes the background, making the heart seem fuller and in the foreground of the picture, despite the fact that it is lighter in color.

Left: For a classical feel try mixing opus regulatum and opus musivum. Here the opus musivum that outlines the heart shape reinforces and strengthens the curvaceous design, while producing a soft and gentle feel.

Below: Here, the heart is made to appear flatter by the use of large tiles in opus regulatum. The opus circumactum in the background has an almost undulating effect.

126

Don't forget interstices

Interstices are the spaces in between the tesserae, and they play an important part in the make-up of the mosaic and the overall feeling of the work. The texture and color of grout used to fill the interstices can change the effect of the mosaic dramatically, and this is something that should be considered carefully when planning the design.

127

Be consistent

Andamento choices are about introducing a system to your work. Once you have decided how the andamento will flow in your piece, it is important to be consistent. Like all systems of rules, it may provide restrictions, but it also allows a kind of freedom within its boundaries.

Left: The main field of the design is laid in lines that run all the way through the objects, from side to side. This is not a typical mosaic way of working, and there is no special name for it. It gives a flat, harmonious quality to a finished surface. If you are going to work like this, you have to be very disciplined about making your cuts run along the lines.

Andamento project: Letters

Mosaics provide a wonderful way to interpret lettering to make really distinctive signs for a house or business. This project demonstrates how different andamento treatments—in this case opus palladianum and opus regulatum—can completely alter the appearance and impact of letters of the same style.

This example shows an old-fashioned style of lettering reminiscent of the theater posters and café signs of nineteenth-century Paris, but you'll come across any number of suitable typefaces by looking in newspapers, magazines, and on the Internet.

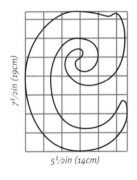

7½in (19cm)

5½in (14cm)

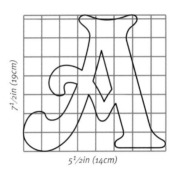

7½in (19cm)

5½in (14cm)

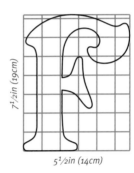

7½in (19cm)

5½in (14cm)

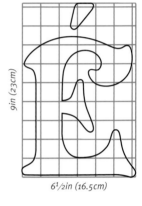

9in (23cm)

6½in (16.5cm)

Palette

Lemon   Red

Lilac

You will need

Household ceramic tiles

Paper for transferring the design

Pen to mark the tiles

Tile nippers

Adhesive and gluing tools

Grout and grouting tools

▲ *To scale and transfer the design, follow the techniques described on pages 78–79. This project has been photographed working on a white substrate and without using glue, to more clearly illustrate the techniques described.*

▶ **1** | Two different tile cuts and ways of laying them are used here. The letters "C" and "F" look like an arbitrary fill of triangular and jagged tile pieces. The letters "A" and "E" have been given a very different treatment, with a neatly laid, flowing square fill of mainly opus regulatum. The fill is largely made up of square tiles that follow the flow and shape of the letter. Precut a stock of tesserae, bearing in mind that you will still have to cut these further to fit as you work.

 128

Find a font

An easy way to see what your lettering or numbering will look like in various fonts is to type the text into a computer and then copy it several times using fonts from your word-processing program. Once you find a font you are happy with, increase to the size you need and print. Instant pattern!

129

What works?

Bold lettering like this—particularly with its flowing, brushstroke design—is an ideal starting point, but blocky, rectangular letters work equally well, although straight edges require a little more patience. Thin, spindly letter shapes are best avoided at first.

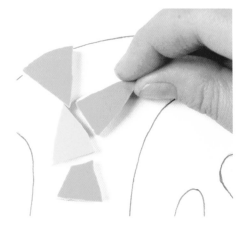

▼ **3 |** Mark the tiles individually to fit the edges of the letters and nibble to the required shape.

▲ **2 |** Take your time arranging the tiles over the letter shapes. Don't worry if your cut shapes overlap the edges of the letter, these can be cut later, when you are happy with the arrangement. Laying opus palladianum is not as easy as it looks—it's a bit like making up a jigsaw puzzle.

▲ The letters can be completed by gluing and grouting using the direct method (see pages 114–116). You can clearly see the varying effects created by use of different opus. The letters are also changed by the choice of grout color (see Consider color: Grout, pages 96–99). Using yellow grout on the "C" makes the piece lighter and busier. Using lavender grout completely changes the relative areas of the two colors to make the "F" more unified. The gray grout on the "A" holds the overall shape of the letter together, improving legibility at a distance. A white grout, on the other hand, makes the pattern of the "E" stand out, fracturing the appearance while adding interest and movement to the letterform.

Tips for laying tesserae

The way in which tiles are laid expresses a mood or gives a sense of animation or calm to a mosaic. Creating flowing curves from small, hard-edged tiles is a challenge that, once overcome, will allow you to take your mosaic work in many rewarding directions. With practice, you can learn to cut tesserae so they fit together into smooth curved shapes, allowing you to attempt designs that are not limited to hard, geometric patterns and fills.

 130

Space evenly

Whatever the size of your tesserae, if you desire an organized or linear look, you need to make sure the space between the tesserae is even. While you can draw a grid to help you place your tesserae correctly, it is a better idea to try to do it by eye, checking the vertical and horizontal alignment and pushing the tesserae gently with your fingers to make fine adjustments.

Tesserae must not be too far apart, nor too close together. In time, you will learn what is pleasing and looks right.

This is the wrong way to lay tesserae (exaggerated). The uneven gaps distract from the design and the effect does not hold together.

 131

Leave gaps for grout

It may sound obvious, but sometimes in the excitement of creating a work of art, the obvious is overlooked. Whichever method of work you employ (see Chapter 4, pages 112–129), remember to leave gaps between the tiles for grouting later. These should be wide enough to accommodate enough grout to surround and support each tile piece, but should not be so wide that the finished design appears fragmented, with the tile pieces floating in a sea of grout. You will learn the right balance through practice.

JARGON BUSTER • INTERSTICES
The spaces or intervals separating the tesserae that can play an integral part of the final mosaic design.

 TRY IT

132 **Drawing parallel curved lines**
To help you plan and lay out a curved line, try drawing parallel curved lines. One way to do this accurately is to use two pencils taped together, with another pencil, a matchbox, or some other object acting as a spacer in between. The aim, of course, is to make the distance between the pencil heads as close as possible to the thickness of the tesserae.

Left: "Drag" the pencils and use your wrist to describe the curve, so that the lines remain parallel.

133

How to lay curves

A curve in mosaic works by "dovetailing" the tesserae together—this usually means cutting every side of your tesserae. The outside of the curve is always longer than the inside, so you need to cut each tessera so that the sides that fit together are wedge-shaped to make the bottom and top shorter or longer, depending on where the tessera fits on the curve.

With a wiggly line, the inside and outside will alternate, so the shape of each "wedge" will vary. It is also often necessary to nibble the top and bottom of the tesserae to follow more closely the line of the curve and to reduce the stepped effect that occurs if you leave the tesserae straight.

Right: *This is not a good curve. The tesserae seem to be arguing with each other and no attempt has been made to cut the edges to fit together. When grouted, the joins will appear uneven and completely break up the flow of the curve.*

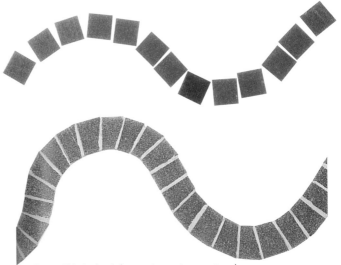

Left: *Carefully cut tesserae fit together to describe the delicate curves of the seahorse's spine, tail, and abdomen.*

Above: *This is the right way to create a neat and flowing curve. Each wedge shape joins not only with an even grout line, but with the line always close to a right angle with the curve so that the grout lines seem to "sit up" and follow each other through the ribbon, rather than cut across and fragment the curve. Each tessera is cut evenly on both sides, so it tapers toward the narrowest edge.*

TRY IT

Practice makes perfect
134 Creating the curved line is one of the most difficult techniques to master. Cut yourself up a pile of tesserae and just practice. Using the parallel-line drawing detailed on page 58, you can master exactly how each tessera fits snugly to the next. If you don't want to waste mosaic materials, use construction paper cut into tesserae shapes.

135

Your grout intention

Kyra Bell's *My Little Duckling* mosaic provides a good example of the "intentional" grout line, because the grout defines the feathers of the duck. The background tesserae are laid in an organized grid, and although grout lines are used in two totally different ways, the artist has achieved a unified whole.

136

Discover interesting patterns

Many interesting surface effects can be achieved by cutting the tiles into special shapes that fit well together. As you gain control of your cutting tools, and they become as versatile as scissors, try cutting ambitious shapes and laying exciting backgrounds or details.

FIX IT

137 Know when to stop

When laying curves or radiating tiles, remember that once you have produced a slightly odd cut, the next tiles are forced into increasingly odd angles by it. Discard any oddly cut tiles and start again.

Randomly curved shapes give a lovely organic, rather scaly impression.

To vary the effect of organic shapes, and to speed up the process, you can include some squares. It can be useful to combine different shapes, since you are often left with some strange-shaped spaces when cutting and laying these tiles.

These honeycomb shapes are rather difficult to cut, but give a wonderful pattern.

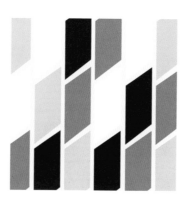

Long two-angled cuts like these are useful as patterns in themselves, but they also help create a feathery impression.

138

Experiment on paper

The ways in which you can construct a single form are almost infinite, as this leaf shape illustrates. There is no single right way to do it. Different ways of cutting and laying create a variety of impressions, and it is up to you to decide what is appropriate for the mosaic you are producing. It can be very useful, therefore, to try out a variety of ideas on paper, before you get busy with the nippers.

This arrangement makes a more obvious reference to a central stem.

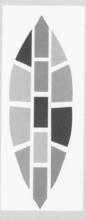

139

Radiating tiles

To make tiles radiate out from a central point you need to cut each tessera on both sides into "keystone" shapes. It can be difficult to make angled cuts that express the way the tiles move round the circle, in which case you may find it helpful to make a plan on paper, dividing up the space geometrically with a ruler.

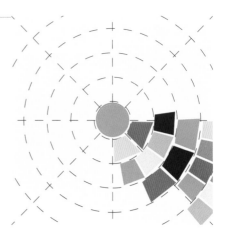

The leaf here has been conventionally treated. Note that the bottom is laid slightly differently to the top. The single tile at the top is a very satisfactory leaf-tip, while the two cut tiles at the bottom help to suggest a stem.

This arrangement suggests the symmetry and skeleton of a leaf. It is a pleasing effect, but would be difficult to achieve if the leaf were large, since it requires long cuts from a whole tile.

This approach refers to a central stalk and also divides the shape skeletally.

This way of laying a leaf might be useful if you wanted to suggest movement.

Providing you are disciplined about laying your tesserae precisely to the outside of the shape, this can be a quick way of forming a leaf.

Laying curves project: Sailboat

This is a deceptively challenging project that requires the raw materials of mosaic—hard, angular tesserae—to be turned into soft, flowing curves. Every element of the design, from the waves to the billowing sail, requires not just the careful cutting of individual tiles, but also the cutting of a sequence of tiles that fit seamlessly together.

12in (30cm)

9½in (24cm)

▲ To scale and transfer the design, follow the techniques described on pages 78–79. This project has been photographed working on a white baseboard and without using glue, to more clearly illustrate the techniques described.

Palette

Sky blue

Dark red

Black

Dark brown

Bright white

Palest pink

You will need

Vitreous glass tesserae

Three millefiori beads

Paper for transferring the design

Pen or grease pencil to mark the tiles

Wheel cutters or tile nippers

Adhesive and gluing tools

Grout and grouting tools

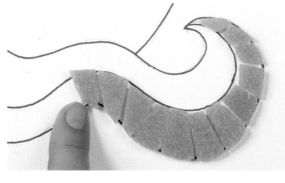

▲ 1 ❘ The first step is to carefully cut the tesserae to fit the curves. The whole design rests on the curve of the waves, so start by completing these before you sit the boat on them. The key is to cut the pieces to flow, and the core technique is "dovetailing" the tesserae around the curves.

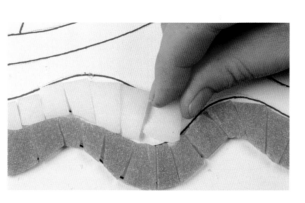

▲ 2 ❘ Make sure the tesserae edge is longer on the outside edge of the curve and shorter on the inside. That way, the tiles seem to expand and contract through the flow of the curve in an organic way, rather than distract from the flow if cut and positioned in a more random way.

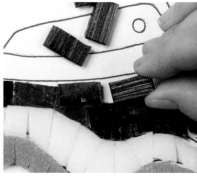

▲ 3 ❘ Lay the tesserae for the hull. Sparkling brown tiles give the effect of varnished wood. Achieve the effect of the individual planks by concentrating on the horizontal curves, just as you did with the waves.

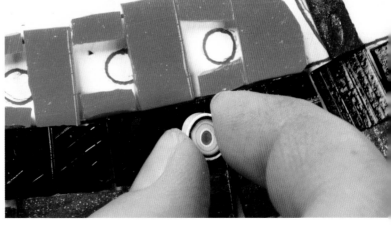

◀ **4** ❘ Use a pen or grease pencil to mark the rounded ends of the bow of the boat to ensure accurate cutting.

▲ **5** ❘ Keep the cabin and portholes simple by leaving square apertures in which to place the millefiori portholes.

Cut the tesserae for the mast with tapering ends.

The curved shape of the bands of tesserae depict the sail full of wind.

▲ **6** ❘ The mast needs to be kept thin and elegant. Take extra care to match each section and to taper the ends to give a flowing, bowed shape. Careful cutting should allow you to get three slivers from a single tile with which to make the mast.

▲ **7** ❘ Three carefully placed, vertically curved bands emphasize the full shape of the sail in a way that a random fill of tiles would not achieve.

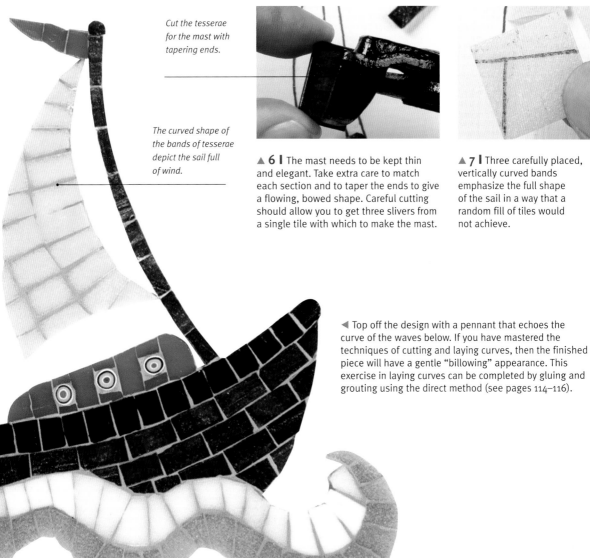

◀ Top off the design with a pennant that echoes the curve of the waves below. If you have mastered the techniques of cutting and laying curves, then the finished piece will have a gentle "billowing" appearance. This exercise in laying curves can be completed by gluing and grouting using the direct method (see pages 114–116).

Templates: Under the sea

Fish provide one of the most popular themes
to be found in mosaic art, from ancient Roman
bathhouses to modern-day swimming pools.
Their streamlined contours are endlessly
satisfying, and the sheer variety in size,
shape, and color gives much scope to
the imagination.

A

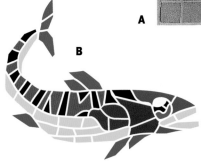

B

140

Study your subject

If your subject matter is a
shell, then study a real
shell. Keep a few in your
work area and learn to
appreciate the texture and
color variations.

141

Exotic fish ◀

This beautiful fish is composed of only a few
tesserae, but they work extremely hard and
the curves of the fish are not sacrificed in the
process. The colors used vary dramatically
in tone—black and white, for example—and
different hues are also utilized, so there
is a lot going on. The alternative follows the
same formula, few tesserae and plenty of
color interest.

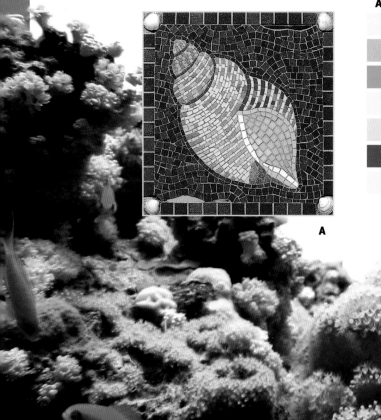

A

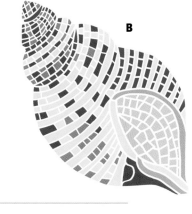

B

142

Seashell ▲

Naturally soft, gentle shades on this
seashell mosaic are strengthened by
deep red touches. The andamento is
very expressive here, caressing and
complementing the rounded structure of
the shell. The alternative version utilizes
lots of murky, mollusklike greens, but
retains the subtlety of the original.

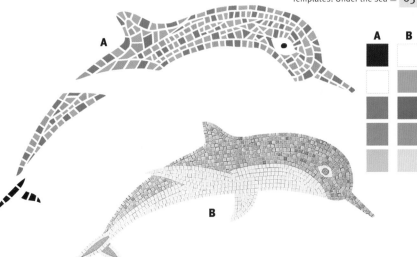

143

Dolphin ►

Dolphins have long been a favorite theme of mosaicists, and this one is a classic, taking full advantage of the beautiful, smooth dolphin shape. The back of the dolphin uses mingled shades of brown, and this adds interest as it contrasts with the flat, creamy underside. The orange detail gives an unexpected pop of color to the whole, and the scheme is retained in the variation that uses alternative aquatic colors.

144

Fishing for inspiration

For great inspiration, visit the pet store, look at fish online, and embrace the limitless color variations and possibilities.

145

Tropical fish ▲

The variegated use of color makes this mosaic particularly convincing. Much of the fish is opus palladianum, and made using large pieces of tesserae, some of which have a color change within the tile itself. The fins are well defined by contrasting stripes, and dramatically radiate away from the fish's body. The black and white in the fins is repeated in the central horizontal stripe that divides the body. Above this stripe are warm browns that give the fish some weight, while below, the pale underbelly gleams eerily. With so much variety within one mosaic, it is interesting to note how the gray grout has a unifying effect.

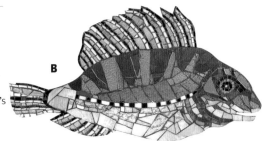

146

Ocean fish ►

Patterned china has been used in this mosaic to help give it texture. Here, only a few different hues have been used, just some blues, two yellows, and white. The drama comes instead from the juxtaposition of light and dark shades: deep blue against pale blue, yellow, and white. The variation uses a more extensive palette, although it still pitches dark colors against light.

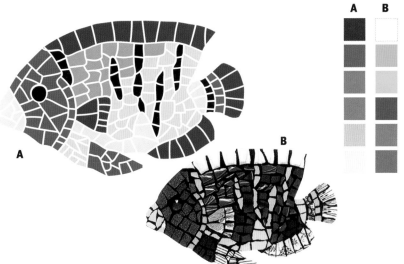

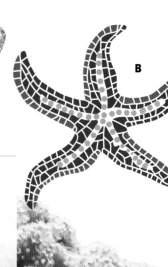

147

Stylized seahorse ▶

The intricate shapes of these gorgeous little creatures provide lots of scope for imaginative use of shaped tesserae and color. The inspired use of triangles on the body and tail adds to the decorative quality, while flashes of bright color add interest. The long streaks in the middle can be made up using smaller tesserae, but try to keep that sharp swerve. The colorful variation is great fun; we are not interested in realism here!

148

Lobster ▼

The complexity of a lobster's form is successfully portrayed in this mosaic. The blues, in opus palladianum, form the body, legs, and claws, while the contrasting red, orange, and white define the details and have some directional movement. The same formula is used in the variation, by pitching ultramarine against murky greens.

149

Placing your creature in an environment

Placing your sea creature in an environment is a fun challenge. The lobster composition is very successful because although the creature is not in a realistic environment, we get the impression that he is staring down at the starfish and the background does not detract from the main subject matter.

150

Starfish ▶

This starfish mosaic has beautiful waving arms depicted in muted coloring. Note how the rounded circular tesserae enhance the decorative effect; a bit difficult to cut, but well worth it. The alternative colorway goes in completely the opposite direction, with eye-opening hues.

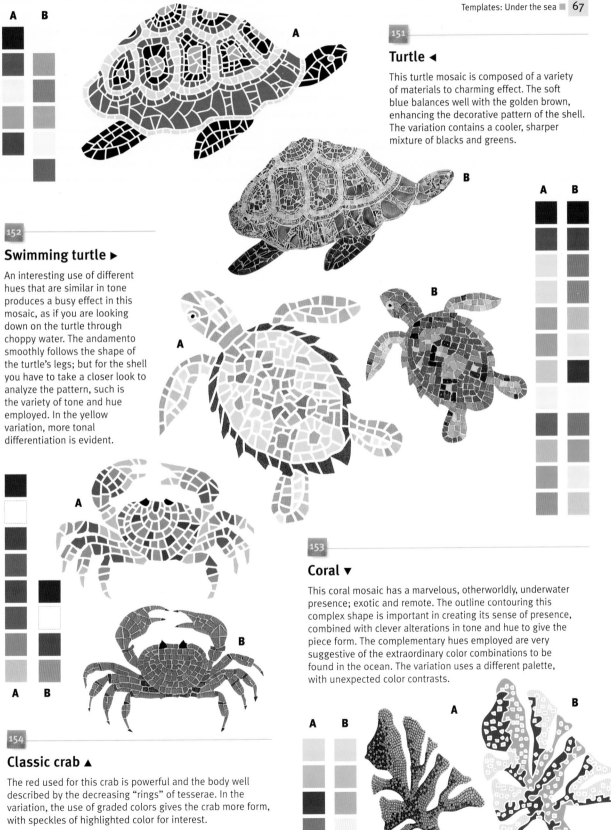

A   B

151

Turtle ◄

This turtle mosaic is composed of a variety of materials to charming effect. The soft blue balances well with the golden brown, enhancing the decorative pattern of the shell. The variation contains a cooler, sharper mixture of blacks and greens.

A

B

152

Swimming turtle ►

An interesting use of different hues that are similar in tone produces a busy effect in this mosaic, as if you are looking down on the turtle through choppy water. The andamento smoothly follows the shape of the turtle's legs; but for the shell you have to take a closer look to analyze the pattern, such is the variety of tone and hue employed. In the yellow variation, more tonal differentiation is evident.

A

B

A   B

153

Coral ▼

This coral mosaic has a marvelous, otherworldly, underwater presence; exotic and remote. The outline contouring this complex shape is important in creating its sense of presence, combined with clever alterations in tone and hue to give the piece form. The complementary hues employed are very suggestive of the extraordinary color combinations to be found in the ocean. The variation uses a different palette, with unexpected color contrasts.

A   B

A

B

A   B

154

Classic crab ▲

The red used for this crab is powerful and the body well described by the decreasing "rings" of tesserae. In the variation, the use of graded colors gives the crab more form, with speckles of highlighted color for interest.

3

Research and plan your design

There are no hard-and-fast rules for designing a mosaic, but there are a number of things to consider carefully before beginning. From the initial source of inspiration through practical planning and considerations of composition and color, the tips in this chapter will help ensure that your design works brilliantly in mosaic form.

Find inspiration

Your inspiration for a design can come from almost anywhere: photographs or vacation memorabilia; a collection of postcards; patterns on fabrics; a motif on a piece of china; and, of course, any of the designs, motifs, or color combinations featured in this book.

TRY IT

155 **Keep an inspiration file**
Keeping an inspiration file is a great way of harnessing your sources of inspiration, and making sure they are at hand when you need them. Have a pinboard or keep a folder, box, or scrapbook specifically for mosaic ideas, and use it to collect images and ideas that you stumble across, such as pictures or motifs torn from magazines, postcards, a scrap of material, a piece of giftwrap, or a photograph or doodle that you take or make yourself.

Creating an inspiration pinboard means that you will be able to look at the images you have collected.

156

For the record

As you develop a visual awareness, you will frequently encounter patterns and designs that inspire you. When you do, be sure to make some sort of record—however short—otherwise the idea may be lost for good. Always carry a small notebook with you so you can jot down drawings or notes about anything that suggests ideas for a mosaic. One of the most useful tools can be your camera phone or digital camera. If you see an interesting image, something that inspires you, take a photograph, load these images onto your computer, and print them out for your file.

Nature is an endless source of inspiration. This mosaic was inspired by dogwood blossom. The artist observed the flowers themselves in detail, then looked at a number of visual representations of dogwoods—from fabrics to engravings—in order to refine their design. Seeing how other artists have reduced a three-dimensional form into a two-dimensional picture can be instructive. A number of sketches were drawn before the final composition was decided on and the mosaic making could begin.

157

Look around you

No matter how many times a subject has been looked at, if it genuinely interests you, you will have something new to bring to it. Subjects don't get exhausted by being looked at again and again, they often become richer and more interesting. You start to see things in them that you previously missed, or, having dealt with the subject in mosaic, you start to see the thing itself in a new way.

The world around you is full of natural and manmade objects that can inspire design ideas. Keep your eyes open for inspiration wherever you are.

Above: *There is no need to look at the title* Autumn Leaves *to know you are stepping into fall in this work. The artist, Rhonda Heisler, has so beautifully captured the sense of falling leaves, and the magic of the moment, finding the perfect tones in each piece of stained glass.*

158

Think like a mosaicist

Once you have started to work in mosaic you will begin to notice mosaic-like qualities in all sorts of ordinary objects around you. Try to work out why you are attracted to these objects—because of their color, design, shape, or texture? Once you know why something appeals to you, it will be easier to produce a working design from it. For instance, if the pebbles appeal to you because of their soft, natural colors, then consider making a mosaic from pebbles or from similar colors of riven marble. If the postcards appeal to you because of their bright colors or simplified designs, you could work on a panel for your kitchen or bathroom that uses bright sea-and-sand colors or recreates a beach scene.

159

Think outside of the box

Remember that inspiration need not be too literal. For example, the colors in a picture or a photograph can be breathtaking, suggesting combinations that you might never have thought of. A pattern or shape isolated in the detail of a photograph might inspire a finished piece that has nothing to do with the original context. Look afresh at domestic objects that are close and familiar, or turn to the natural world. Perhaps a section of a machine looks interesting, or a piece of carpet. You might even be inspired by a mood or an atmosphere. Your resulting mosaic design can contain abstract forms or recognizable images, and can have a contemporary or traditional feel to it.

160

Let the medium guide you

You may find that the thing that really drives you is not a particular subject matter, but the mosaic-making process itself. There is an immense amount of interest to be derived from simply investigating what the medium enables you to do. Allow yourself to be led by the colors or textures of the materials, for example, or play about with the different effects created by reflective and matte surfaces, or with cutting contrasts.

Right: Secrets *by Virginia Gardner magically moves the viewer's eyes as millefiori ropes dance across the stained-glass canvas. This is a wonderful example of allowing the medium guide you.*

Above: The Roman mosaics from the Great Palace in Constantinople show scenes from everyday life with remarkable clarity and so are a valuable historical as well as artisic source.

Above: The Dome of the Rock in Jerusalem is the earliest remaining Islamic monument and is remowned for its stunning mosaics, both inside and out.

Above: This multicolored dragon stands at the entrance to Park Güell in Barcelona, just one of Gaudi's striking mosaic contributions to the city and now a UNESCO World Heritage Site.

161

Respect copyright

Whereas artists look to masters for inspiration all the time, it is very important to respect copyright. If you do wish to emulate someone else's work then you must acknowledge that you were inspired by them and you must not claim it as your own original artwork.

162

Turn to the experts

The work of other mosaicists can provide a rich source of inspiration. There are a number of examples in this book alone, and you can also try looking through art and architectural books, visiting your nearest museum, or surfing the Internet. You should also be alert to the many mosaics—old and new—that may decorate shops, offices, and public buildings in your area.

Contemporary mosaic-makers have a tremendous range of art historical sources to draw upon. Examples of ancient Roman mosaics that survive to this day depict everyday life, studies of animals and birds, and abstract border patterns, while in Barcelona the work of Antoni Gaudi explores the idea that mosaics can be enjoyed for purely decorative purposes and not only for representational means, introducing abstract patterns and stylized forms.

163

Find inspiration here

This book features a number of templates, which can be used in a variety of ways. On one level, you can browse through the pages in search of a source of inspiration that will help you design your own mosaic. However, if one mosaic in particular takes your fancy you can replicate more closely. Enlarge the design to the desired size using a photocopier (see Scaling up, pages 78–79). Be aware of the scale: if you want to closely follow the pattern of individual pieces, make sure your chosen tesserae will cut comfortably to the sizes required. The templates are different to the artworks in the book, which should not be copied in this way as they are subject to the artists copyright (see above).

Planning and designing

Translating an idea from the moment of inspiration to the point where it becomes an actual mosaic may seem like a daunting task if you haven't done much of this kind of thing before. Here are a few guidelines you can follow to change any doubts.

TRY IT

164 **Trace out unnecessary detail**
A good exercise in simplifying ideas is to trace your sources of inspiration. Tape some tracing paper over a two-dimensional source—such as a pattern or design found in a magazine or book—then try using a thick felt-tip pen to go over the main outlines. A thick pen will stop you from being too fussy about detail and will help simplify and strengthen the design. Color this tracing, restricting yourself to just three or four colors—again use strong, thick felt-tip pens. You can even "trace the tracing" to simplify and strengthen the design further.

When you are happy with the tracing you can enlarge it as required (see Scaling up, pages 78–79).

Virginia Gardner began with an oil-pastel drawing that worked through all color considerations in advance, making ordering of materials efficient. The mosaic, Allure, is a beautiful interpretation.

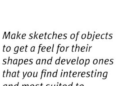

165

Keep it simple

The main principle for adapting source material into a design for a mosaic is to try to simplify things as much as possible. Concentrate on color and shapes, and discard complex details that will be impossible to interpret in mosaic: remember that you are creating a mosaic image rather than a painting or illustration, and concentrating on tiny details will inevitably lead to frustration and probable disappointment.

Analyze exactly what it is that has inspired you, and translate that onto paper. In preliminary sketches, try to refine the subject of your mosaic to its bare essentials. Strong silhouettes are often important in getting the character of your subject across: if the outline can "tell the story" on its own, you will have no problem.

166

Think like a designer

When honing your ideas, keep visual design elements in mind: line, texture, shapes or form, and color. Consider using repetition or rhythm, working with symmetry or asymmetry, and emphasizing the focal point.

Make sketches of objects to get a feel for their shapes and develop ones that you find interesting and most suited to mosaic reproduction.

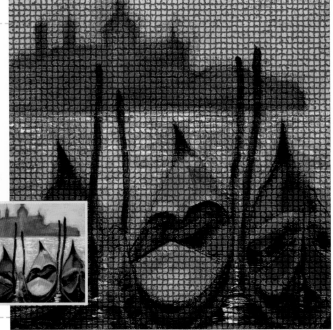

TRY IT

167 **Digital mosaicization**
Several computer programs—Photoshop in particular—feature filters for creating stained-glass and mosaic "looks." You may find it helpful, or at least intriguing, to scan your inspiration image into one of these programs and apply the filter. A particular advantage of working in this way is that you can quickly try different color combinations on your computer screen before embarking on the time and expense of cutting your mosaic materials.

168

Patterns online

If the thought of creating your own mosaic design is daunting, you can buy tried-and-tested mosaic and stained glass patterns from the Internet, either individually or in books. These are usually simple designs that you can use to jump-start your creativity. A bought pattern, like a cartoon, will assist you in determining the amount of materials you will need.

169

Make a cartoon

You may already be a budding artist, and there is great satisfaction to be had by translating an original design into mosaic. Perhaps you paint, or prefer to draw, but whatever your preference, the end goal for a mosaic design is to create a "cartoon"—a simple line drawing used to determine materials, color relationships, and overall look.

Creating a cartoon, or working drawing, enables you to solve potential composition problems and will help you estimate the materials required. It does not have to be a detailed drawing, more like a drawing you might find in a child's coloring book.

Coloring the cartoon is also important. In painting, you can mix red and white and get pink, but most mosaic materials have a fixed color palette. Although distance from the work will allow some visual color blending, in smaller projects it is unlikely you will realize this effect. Planning the color fields helps create a color scheme best suited to your design.

Once you are happy with your color cartoon, trace or copy the primary lines of the original with thin black lines, ready for scaling by grid or photocopier (see pages 78–79).

The original sketch was made while on vacation in Italy.

The first cartoon has been rejected, since the iconic Tuscan trees are out of proportion, and the sky and mid-field area is too large in relationship to the rest of the drawing.

The taller, thinner trees and sweeping fields are graceful. The trees on top of the hill and a smaller sky area make a more interesting composition that would translate well to mosaic.

The final outline can be enlarged to any size using a photocopier or by hand.

170
Will it work?

Once you have an idea of what you wish to make a mosaic of, be it realistic or abstract, try making small prototypes like those above—this is especially helpful if your planned mosaic is large. By making small, to-scale versions you can experiment with different color combinations, materials, and cutting styles.

171
Paper tesserae

A good and cheap way to plan your cutting is to make a small, to-scale prototype using construction paper. The act of cutting individual tesserae out of paper may sound silly, but the exercise will help you understand exactly how you need to cut your mosaic materials. This is especially helpful with details such as eyes in portraits.

TRY IT

172
Stick it up
If you have concerns as to whether a planned mosaic will work in a specific location—is it the right size? Are the colors pleasing?—try hanging your colored cartoon in its intended position. Leave it there for a few days and "live" with the artwork.

173
Think site specific

Think about where the finished mosaic is going to be placed and whether it will be suitable for that particular environment. If your mosaic is to be a self-contained "picture," there is no need to take account of any environmental factors. If, however, it is to be installed in a specific site, then it should be designed with reference to the architecture and color scheme that it is destined to become a part of. For example, if your mosaic is going to be sited in a small room, do not make it too large or busy—a certain amount of distance between the mosaic and the viewer is necessary, so that the viewer can see the mosaic as a whole, not just as a mass of individual tesserae.

Remember also that different types of tesserae have their own qualities, with some more suitable for certain projects than others, both aesthetically and practically (see Go compare, pages 38–39).

Nebula Aqua *is an installation in a private home. It is a series of six "Nebula," integrating mineral specimens, semiprecious stones, smalti, and more. Artist Sonia King designed the elements of the installation to move around the curved wall and "float" down the staircase.*

174

Make a site pattern

When your mosaic is to be sited in a particular place, you may need to work around certain fixed objects. In which case, to be sure that your mosaic will slot exactly into place, gather lots of brown paper and make a life-size pattern of the area—a paper template that represents the perimeter of the area you wish to cover in mosaic.

A bathroom floor is a good example, because you will need to work around fixed pieces of sanitary ware. The whole area of the floor will not fit on a single piece of brown paper, so the template will have to be constructed from several sheets of paper, stuck together with masking tape.

The difficulty with any pattern comes with curves, which are more challenging to measure precisely. The secret of making successful patterns around curved areas is to be unafraid of cutting away too much paper, since it is easy to patch paper back in.

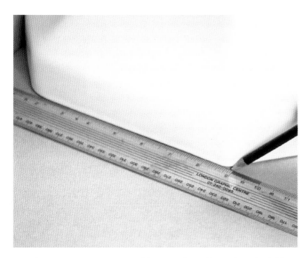

1 I Where you encounter an object, such as the pedestal of this basin, measure out its position and dimensions so you can mark them onto brown paper. The outer dimensions of the front and sides of this pedestal are easy to measure. The angles at the corner of this pedestal were quite easy to measure but, had they not been, they could have been made by cutting out the general shape of the pedestal and then patching pieces of paper back in to fit the shape.

TRY IT

175 **Virtual location**
Using Photoshop or a similar computer program, try "placing" your cartoon in its environment to see if the planned size and color combinations will work.

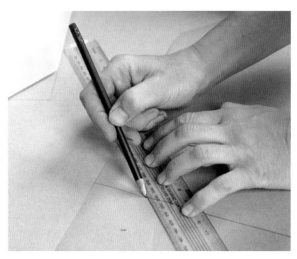

2 I Once you have the outer dimensions of the object, draw them onto the matte side of the brown paper. To draw angled sections of a template, measure from the corners of the general outline to the point where the object ends and transfer these measurements onto the brown paper. Then cut out the area where the object stands.

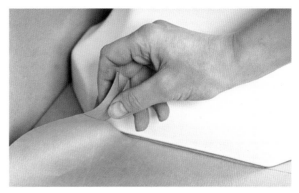

3 I Place the brown paper in position in order to check the accuracy of your template. If the space left for the object is too small, cut more away with a craft knife. If the space is too big, make a patch so that it does fit precisely. You can now use this template to accurately plan your design.

176

Working out scales of enlargement

To work out by what percentage you should enlarge on a photocopier or how large your scaling-by-hand squares need to be:

1 Measure one side of the original and the length you want this side to be enlarged to.

2 Divide the enlarged measurement by the original measurement: this gives you the factor of enlargement—the amount by which you must multiply any measurement from the original to find out the size it will be on the enlargement.

> For example:
> Width of original
> = 6in (15cm)
> Width of enlargement
> = 30in (75cm)
> 30 ÷ 6 = 5
> (75 ÷ 15 = 5)
> Factor of enlargement
> = 5

> For example:
> Factor of enlargement
> = 5
> 5 × 100 = 500
> Percentage enlargement
> = 500%

Enlargement by percentage

To enlarge a drawing on a photocopier, you need to know the percentage value of the enlargement. To do this, move the decimal two places to the right. This gives you the percentage needed to enlarge the sketch.

> For example:
> Original grid square
> = ½in (1cm)
> Factor of enlargement
> = 5
> ½ (1) × 5 = 2½ (5)
> Enlargement grid square
> = 2½in (5cm)

Scaling by hand

Multiply the size of a grid square on the original by the factor of enlargement to give the grid square size for the enlargement.

177

Scaling up

Once you have your finalized line drawing, you may need to enlarge it to fit the final size of your mosaic. The easiest way to do this is with a photocopier, although you can also use a grid technique to enlarge your motif by hand.

Using a photocopier
Many home printers have photocopy features, or visit a local library or print shop, where you can pay a small fee to use a photocopier. Some larger copy centers have photocopiers that can make copies up to 36in (90cm) wide.

1 I The copying process can lighten the design slightly, so it is worth going over the original with a dark felt-tip pen to strengthen the outlines.

2 I Measure your original and work out the percentage increase required (see Working out scales of enlargement, left). Place the original face down on the photocopier glass and enter the percentage enlargement in the control panel. If your design will not fit onto one piece of paper when enlarged, simply rotate the original and make a copy of the second part—to do this more than once, treat the original as four corners, each of which needs to be enlarged. You may even need to copy the copies to reach the desired enlargement—in which case, measure the interim copy and use the same calculation to work out the second percentage enlargement.

Enlarging by hand

1 | To enlarge by hand you need to draw two grids of squares, the first to fit over your original design and the second, with the same number of squares, to fit the required enlargement.

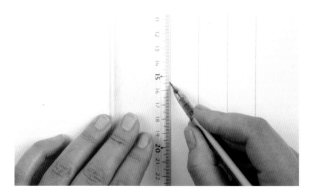

2 | Measure the original and work out the required scale of enlargement (see Working out scales of enlargement, page 78). Draw the second grid onto a piece of tracing paper, or directly onto your substrate if you plan to use the direct method of working (see pages 114–116). To copy the drawing, go to the original and choose one of the main lines or features of the design. Look carefully at where and in which square the line begins in the original, then mark the same place in the second grid with a dot. Follow the line to see where it crosses each line in the first grid, and draw a dot in the corresponding place in the second grid.

TRY IT

178 **Graph paper**
Draw your original design directly onto graph paper to make scaling easier.

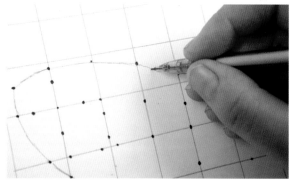

3 | Join these dots to complete the line of the original. Check visually to make sure the original line and your copy look the same—it is easy, particularly at first, to get a dot in the wrong place.

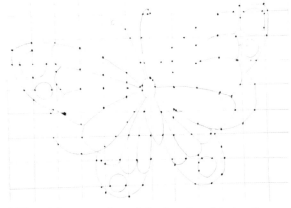

4 | Repeat the process for each line from the original, until you have a copy of the whole design on the large grid.

TRY IT

179 **Use a proportion wheel**
A proportion wheel will help you determine the percent you must increase your cartoon by to photocopy to the size of your chosen substrate. Adjust the inner wheel to the current size of the artwork, and the outer wheel to the size of your substrate. The center window will then give you the percent you need to photocopy by.

Planning project: Checked pattern

This is an ideal piece to practice the basic techniques of working in vitreous glass tiles, scaling your design, and learning to position the cut tiles over the drawing on the substrate. Yet it is also a piece that allows endless variations and adaptation, despite using the most basic cuts. The design is based around a simple square grid.

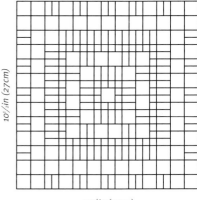

10½in (27cm)

10½in (27cm)

Scale the design (see pages 78–79) and transfer it directly onto the substrate, following the technique described on page 115, and the advice given in Step 1, below.

Palette

Ice blue   Orange

Copper   Sky blue

Pale lilac   Pearlescent pink

Pale Pearlescent pink

You will need

Vitreous glass tesserae

Ruler

Pen

Wheel cutter or tile nippers

Adhesive and gluing tools

Grout and grouting tools

▲ **1** | Using a ruler, draw up the outside square on your substrate. If you are following this design exactly, it will be 13 tile squares high and the same number wide. Then draw in the diagonals from corner to corner to find the exact center of the design. Finally, lightly draw in the vertical and horizontal center lines.

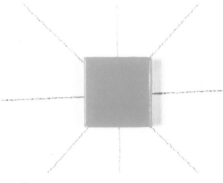

▲ **2** | Start in the center. Place a whole tile at the intersection of the center lines. Position this exactly by eye, or by drawing diagonals across the tile.

▲ **3** | Surround the center tile with quarter-cut tiles.

180

The tile square

Each square of the grid should be slightly larger than the size of the tiles you are using, to allow for grout. As a guide, add approximately ⅟₃₂in (1mm) to each side of a standard ¾in (2cm) tile. This measurement is called the tile square.

▲ **4 |** Most of the tiles in this design do not need to be cut at all. The other cuts are simple. Here, the tile is simply split into two halves.

▲ **6 |** Position a row of quarter-cut blue tiles to provide a frame within a frame.

▲ **5 |** As you continue to work outward, the grid remains important. Start each row at the center lines and lay the tiles to the corners, adjusting their spacing.

▶ To complete the project using the direct method (see pages 114–116), fix the tiles in place and grout. The finished piece is a smart and eye-catching design that relies heavily on accurate planning and scaling of the grid. The copper tiles add a great finishing touch.

Composition considerations

Composition is the way the elements of a picture or design are placed and arranged, and is used to achieve balance and harmony through the positioning and sizing of the various components. In order to execute a successful composition the mosaic artist should consider the positioning of the various motifs, as well as backgrounds, borders, light sources, and how to focus the viewer.

TRY IT

 Focus the viewer

When planning your composition, you may choose to provide the viewer with a path for the eye to follow. The positioning of elements that lead the viewer through an image can be strong or subtle. Sometimes an image will work to a rigid grid onto which key elements are placed exactly. For example, a design might be divided into thirds, with key elements positioned on some of the intersections of the imaginary dividers between each third. The path may be created by using lines or boundaries between areas of different tones and colors that guide the eye, or it may work more subtly through positioning elements—such as spots of color—that act as stepping stones to guide you through the picture.

181 **Set up a still life**

If planning a composition on paper doesn't work for you, try making your own still life. Play around with arrangements of objects, trying them in different positions in relation to each other. When you hit upon a happy balance, make a drawing, or take a digital photograph, to use as the basis of your design.

The composition in this arrangement is somewhat unbalanced. The pink bottle is "lost" within the outline of the clear jug.

This arrangement fails because the blue jar, lying on its side, steers the eye out of the frame. The remaining objects are separated from the jar and positioned in too orderly an array.

Positioning the largest item at the front is not a good idea since this means the supporting objects are lost or hidden from view.

This is a better composition. The objects are grouped more naturally, and the shapes interlock.

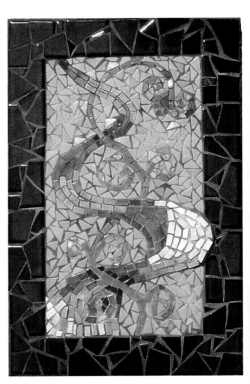

Above: The construction of a path that manipulates the viewer's gaze is perhaps the most controlling compositional technique.

Left: In Becoming, *by Carol Shelkin, the two-toned background gracefully draws the viewer to focus on the main subject, the girl drinking.*

183

Cut and paste ideas

One way of composing a design is to draw the elements on separate pieces of paper and move them around, experimenting with different combinations. This enables you to see alternative compositions that might work.

Once you have a composition you are happy with, tape the pieces to your work surface and trace the drawing, then transfer it to your substrate in the usual way. To see the final composition, see page 91.

Some compositions definitely won't work—here all the elements have been positioned too far to the left, making the picture look unbalanced.

Here, the various elements seem vertically disconnected, and isolated. What is needed is a more cohesive feel to the piece.

Centering all the elements, however, can make the design too crowded and weaken the "framing" of the picture.

Be creative with backgrounds and simple themes

The background should be thought of as a key part of the whole mosaic piece, rather than simply an empty area that needs to be filled in order to complete the mosaic. Think of the variety of background texture you can create with a pencil—by crosshatching or sketching in different directions, building up a description of form through thicker and thinner, darker and lighter lines—and translate this to your mosaic design. When you are producing mosaics with large areas of background, it is worth carrying out experiments to decide on a suitable background treatment. Some designs can bear quite a strong tonal and color field, while for others a strong background would be far too dominating. Suit your approach to the requirements of the design. One of the most enjoyable aspects of inventing new background treatments is that you can give a free rein to your instinct to be playful.

The simple theme can be infinitely varied. Once you have come up with an idea, be prepared to pursue it; often it does require a bit of work to discover what can really be done with it. Here, the basic theme has been worked to make the color contrasts bolder but the distortion of shape more subtle.

This practice panel illustrates how you can give interest to a repeating pattern through minute distortions. The curved lines that the color changes follow, and the wavy distortion created by using tiles of slightly differing shapes and sizes, make the basic geometric pattern appear to flow like fabric.

FIX IT

Border balance

185 Borders can complete a composition, and help to balance out the visual structure of the mosaic. When choosing the design and colors for a border, remember that it is there to support and show off the main attraction in the central part of the design, therefore beware of making a border so bright and jazzy that it competes with what is happening in the middle (unless you are making a mirror frame, in which case you can go for it). In particular, resist the "traffic light" urge—repetition of a sequence of two or three bright colors—since it rarely works. On the other hand, the border ought not to be too wishy-washy or insubstantial either. Tonally, it should carry some weight, and form an integral part of the balance of your composition.

The border in this mosaic is well balanced with the central motif—the border is interesting in its own right, but does not detract from the main composition.

Play with pattern

Pattern is in the nature of mosaic, since any design that is made up through a series of minute pieces must have pattern as one of its essential elements. It is easy to sideline the effects of pattern, but if you play on what the material does naturally it is easy to produce exciting results.

Above: *The semiabstract nature of this landscape,* Mosman, *by Marian Shapiro, uses pattern in a sophisticated way. Some sections have formal and realistic patterns, such as the overlapping foliage on the left. Other areas have more random lines within them and informal patterns. The mix of materials (vitreous glass, fused glass, beach glass, smalti, and unglazed ceramic) also creates a patterned effect. Notice how the seagulls help convey the effect of an aerial view of the coastline.*

Above: *The background of* Big Steps, *by Irit Levy, is composed of a slightly irregular pattern of brick shapes, which gives additional motion to what is already a wonderfully moving artwork. Materials: marble, unglazed ceramic, glass, and millefiori.*

Above: *This beautiful stained-glass mosaic,* Encoded, *by Rhonda Heisler, is a series of panels that together illustrate repetitive patterning. The tones used help distinguish one pattern from the next, and this is an excellent example of how rhythm can be conveyed.*

187

Look to the light

The way light and shade is depicted in a mosaic is especially effective in giving a sense of form to an object, therefore, in order to achieve realistic representations in your mosaics, it is useful to have a basic understanding of how light works.

A single directional light source, such as from a window or lightbulb, will always create the most light on the surface of the object closest to the light, with the darkest part of the shadow behind the opposite side of the object. In between, there will be a range of midtones that vary according to the amount of light falling on the surface.

Understanding light and shadow
If the object or light source is moved in relation to the other, the highlight and shadows will also move, as can be seen here. As the light is moved, the shadow underneath the egg and the highlight on the top surface of the egg move in opposite directions—the shadow away from the light source, the highlight toward it.

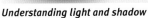
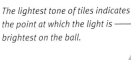

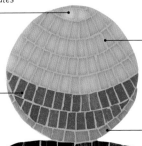

The lightest tone of tiles indicates the point at which the light is brightest on the ball.

This part of the ball is still light, but not as brightly lit as the top highlight.

The darkest tone of tiles indicates where the ball is most in shadow.

This midtone indicates where some reflected light is illuminating this part of the ball.

The shadow cast by an overhead light source is small.

Overhead light source diagram
When the light source is directly above an object—in this case a ball—the highlight is on the top. The "footprint" of the shadow is very small—just as it is when the sun is overhead.

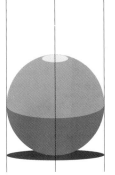

Overhead light source mosaic
In this simple mosaic of the ball, the different areas of light and shadow have been exaggerated. Resist the temptation to use black tiles to create a "proper" shadow: the end result often looks flat and dead (here, the left side of the shadow has been tiled in black tiles, the right in brown, so that you can compare the finished result).

TRY IT

188 **Posterizing an image**
Posterization is a technique for simplifying the number of tones in a photographic image, and it is a great way to ascertain where areas of light and shade are brightest and darkest. This digital method can be carried out using any simple photo-editing software program using a scanned photo or a copyright-free image from the Internet.

1 I Open a digital photograph or scanned picture in the software program. Save a copy of the image as a black-and-white or grayscale image.

2 I Turn the brightness and contrast controls up to 100 percent—the image will turn completely white and disappear.

3 I Leaving the contrast at 100 percent, slowly lower the brightness so that the features of the image begin to reappear.

Oblique light source diagram
To construct the shadows in a design, first decide where the source of light is, then draw parallel lines from that source to show where the edges of the shadow will be.

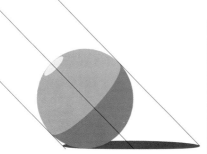

Oblique light source mosaic
In this version of the ball, the light is falling obliquely from the side. You can see how the shape of the shadow and the position of the highlight have changed from the overhead light example. You can also see a slightly lighter area on the side of the ball that is in shadow where some reflected light is faintly illuminating that side of the ball.

The lightest tone of tiles indicates the point at which the light is brightest on the ball.

The darkest tone of tiles indicates where the ball is most in shadow.

This midtone indicates where some reflected light is illuminating this part of the ball.

This part of the ball is still light, but not as brightly lit as the top highlight.

The shadow cast by an oblique light source is wider than that cast by an overhead source.

189

Drop shadow

A drop shadow is the rough image cast by an object blocking rays of illumination. This is beautifully illustrated in *Vespucci*, by George Fishman, made using smalti and split-faced stone tesserae. The shadow of the sails on the water, which makes the mosaic especially realistic, is indicated using darker blue tesserae than the actual water.

4 I Play around with the brightness level until the features are strongly defined, then save the image under another name (so that you can still use the original image if you want to go back and change it). Print and scale (see pages 78–79) your high-contrast picture to give the outline of the dark and light areas.

The Statue of Liberty mosaic uses just two tones of green to convey the falling of light onto the statue. It is a simple but very effective technique that can be applied to many projects.

Mural project: Jungle menagerie

This project is a large picture that brings together many of the techniques covered in the book. It is also a piece in which composition is key—the animals are separate elements that you can reposition, repeat, or even substitute with other animals/elements that you find elsewhere. Because it has a flat, almost cartoonlike feel, don't worry too much about the size of each piece in relation to the next one. What is important is to get an overall balance to the piece.

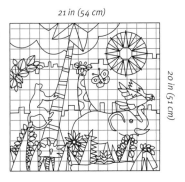

Scale the design (see pages 78–79) and transfer it directly onto the substrate, following the technique described on page 115.

21 in (54 cm)

20 in (51 cm)

You will need

Household ceramic tiles

Millefiori beads

Pebbles

Stick-on googly eye (optional)

Prepared substrate

Pen

Tile cutter

Tile nippers

PVA glue, spatula, and fine paintbrush

Grout, squeegee, and sponge

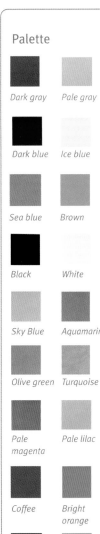

Palette

Dark gray	Pale gray
Dark blue	Ice blue
Sea blue	Brown
Black	White
Sky Blue	Aquamarine
Olive green	Turquoise
Pale magenta	Pale lilac
Coffee	Bright orange
Dark green	Emerald green
Yellow	Red

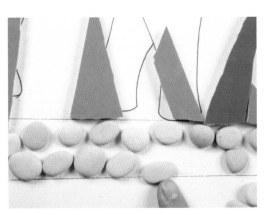

▲ 1 ❘ This project is executed directly (see pages 114–116), and once you have transferred your drawing, the approach to follow is to take one element at a time. You may choose to dry lay then glue on an area-by-area basis, or dry lay the whole mural then glue the pieces down in stages.

Start with the foliage, using large shards of green tiles of different tones. Position these first as the stems, then create the foliage around them. Add the pebbles at the bottom of the picture to provide variation in texture.

▼ 2 ❘ Use various cuts and shapes for the leaves, such as half-moons, small triangles, simple rectangles, and whole leaf shapes.

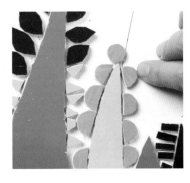

▶ **3 ❘** Make "leaf pairs" from a single leaf shape split in half. Place small circles in between to suggest fruit berries.

▼ **4 ❘** This flower shape (as is much of the picture) is inspired by the work of the French painter Henri Rousseau. The cuts used are simple triangles, semicircles, diamonds, and U-shapes. Keep the placement of the pieces symmetrical.

◀ **5 ❘** For this flower cut a central circle, then position a selection of slim, leaf-shaped fragments for the petals. Keep them large and exuberant, cutting across the bottom petals so they appear to go behind the leaves in the foreground.

▶ **6 ❘** Add an exotic dimension to some of the flowers and foliage using carefully chosen millefiori.

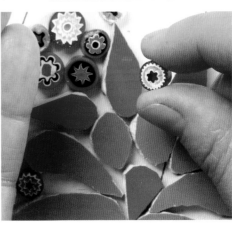

▼ **9 ❘** Next, place the tusk of the elephant, which you must carefully shape from a single piece of white tile. Persist in cutting this as one element because it strengthens the design—you may lose a few attempts to breakage along the way.

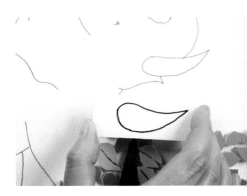

▼ **7 ❘** Use large pieces of green tiles of different tones to create the leaf fronds of the palm tree. A tile cutter will give a strong, clean diagonal line.

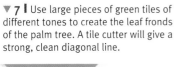

▲ **8 ❘** Use large chunks of brown or maroon tile for the trunk. Concentrate on getting the outside line absolutely straight. The dark bands get thicker toward the bottom of the trunk. At the end of the trunk, cut into the bottom of the tile to create a curve that fits around the flowers and foliage of the foreground.

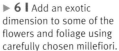

◄ 10 | Create the outline for the elephant's ear using carefully cut rectangular shapes in a darker shade of gray, tapering them at the ends. Fill in the rest of the elephant with triangles and tapered and curved rectangles to suggest the aged, creased feel of the animal's hide. If you are going to use a stick-on googly eye, fill the whole outline, since the eye will be glued on after the whole piece is finished and grouted. If you want to use a piece of millefiori, or a small fragment of tile cut into a circle, you will need to cut the tiles in front of the ear so as to leave a small hole to accommodate the eye.

► 11 | The monkey is a silhouette made up of small square-cut pieces of tile. Again, it's important to get the flow of the back and limbs, creating lines of grout rather than just using a random fill. Shape the face from a single rounded piece—no more detail is needed.

◄ 12 | Use more leaf pairs to add the large branches of foliage that protrude into the picture.

► 13 | Start the sun with a centrally placed octagon of bright orange. For the rays, cut red tiles into strips, then cut these diagonally to create "shards." Square off the bottoms so that each shard is a very thin isosceles triangle. Place them around the center, then fill in between with triangles of yellow, then the remaining gaps with smaller orange pieces.

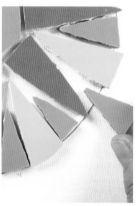

Octagon cutting

To create the octagon shape at the center of the sun, cut a circle, then draw in the arms of a cross and the diagonals in between. Rule across between where each line intersects the circle, and apply your tile cutters along these lines.

► 14 | The giraffe can be tiled any time after you have the body of the elephant in place. Try to get the curve of the neck to rise out of the curve of the elephant's back. The neck should curve gently backward to add to the animal's aloofness. Place the dark tiles first along the outside line of the neck, then fill the spaces in between with cream tiles. Practice cutting the eyes and mouth until you produce the same shape in consistent sizes. These tiles are crucial to creating the heavy-lidded, haughty expression of the animal.

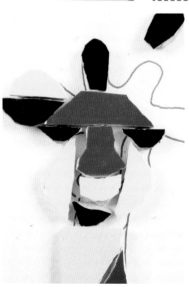

▲ 15 | When the position of the elephant is established in the "background," move on to the parrot. It is important to get the placement of the eye right, as well as the cutting of the hooked, nutcracker beak. You can give added emphasis to the eye by making it protrude slightly above the level of the surrounding tiles. Pad out the back of the tile with extra adhesive or other materials, or, if you are using millefiori, by placing two thinner ones on top of each other.

▼ **16 |** The butterfly is made up of two circles and a concentric fill. Angle the tile pieces so that they dovetail together. Very small circles of black tile have been used to provide the "eyes" at the end of the antennae.

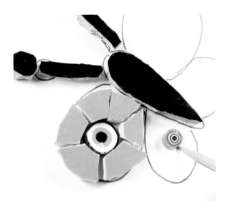

▲ **17 |** Create the clouds in the background using rectangles of the same width but of different heights. The outline of the cloud behind the tree needs to be cut with care to achieve a smooth and continuous outline.

▲ **18 |** The same opus style as the clouds continues into the remainder of the background, giving a regularity and calmness, but without the harshness or monotony of opus regulatum (see page 52). The main background has been banded into different tones of blue to give a sense of recession. You could experiment with mixing the tiles more, but you must be careful not to make the background a distraction. Try to keep the overall effect cool and controlled.

▲ **19 |** Once the glue is dry, grout the mural in the usual way (see page 30).

Consider color: Tesserae

Design, composition, technical competence, and cutting ability are all important aspects of mosaic-making, but one of the most fundamental skills involved in creating a successful mosaic is the use of color. You will find that in mosaic this is not always straightforward, and in order to make the most of the range of effects mosaic can allow, you really need to understand the basics of color theory. Learning to work with colors and exploiting the rich possibilities that the materials offer are important steps in producing good mosaics.

Know your limits: the mosaic palette

The mosaic palette is limited. Although some color mixing is possible (see Optical mixing, right), you cannot mix infinite variations of color in the way that you can with paint. However, you should not regard this as a limitation, but relish the creative challenge it gives you—allow this restriction to force you to find your creative edge, and interesting things will start to happen. Mosaic often thrives on a kind of stylization, in color as well as form. This does not mean that it cannot possess great subtlety and depth, but it does so within its own parameters.

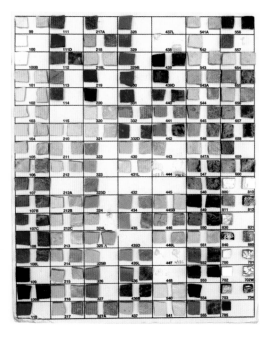

The colors that you can obtain in vitreous glass and smalti range from somber to very bright. Extra interest can be gained by using brightly colored smalti, gold or silver tesserae, or gold-veined vitreous glass tiles.

Learn the language

Color can be regarded as possessing three basic properties: hue, value, and intensity.

Hue

Hue is the term given to a color in its purest form in the color spectrum; blue and yellow, red and purple, for example. Some mosaic materials offer a wider range of hues than others. In the eighteenth century, the Vatican workshops produced literally thousands of different colors, with so wide a range that it was possible for mosaicists to make precise copies of paintings. Today the range is much smaller, and some hues have decidedly limited ranges. For example, yellow is rather inadequately represented; there are one or two mauves, but there is no true purple; and the range of pinks extends to about two. With such limitations you have to rely on using context rather than color to make sense of your mosaic.

Hue is another word for color. Blue, yellow, red, and purple are all hues.

Optical mixing

While colors in mosaic work cannot be mixed in the same way as they can with painting, some optical mixing is possible, since distance allows for fusion of colors. Try working in a pointillist way, mixing colors by mingling their composite hues. Mixing shades of red and blue, for instance, will create the effect of purple when you stand back and view the mosaic.

This mixture of yellows and blues gives an overall impression of green, an optical effect that works best when viewed from a distance.

Value

The value of a color is a description of how light or dark it is, therefore, a blue and a green may be the same value, even though they are different hues. For the purposes of most work in mosaic there are really only three main value divisions: dark, mid, and light. Using contrasting values in areas of a design gives a clearly defined separation, allowing the areas to stand apart from each other. Using similar values makes areas merge, even when the colors are quite different. Value also lends depth to the flat surface of a picture. Conventionally, softer, lighter values suggest greater depth and distance than strong darker elements, which appear to be closer to the viewer.

You will notice, particularly when a mosaic is grouted, that similar values have more in common with one another than similar hues, or similar degrees of intensity. This can have both a beneficial and a problematic consequence. The use of close values can create remarkably subtle effects, but at the risk of losing the clarity of an image.

When similar values of different colors are placed together, the areas appear to merge.

When tiles of different values are used, the areas are far more distinct. The blue triangle appears to advance from the lighter-toned background, while the pink triangle seems to recede from the darker-toned surrounding tiles.

Intensity

Intensity refers to the relative strength or weakness of a color, whether it is bright or muted. A bright tessera will appear all the richer placed next to a muted, heavy color.

The yellow in this piece is distinctly different in intensity of color to the tiles that surround it. It is much brighter than the other colors and stands out dramatically. In a large mosaic you would want to balance the amount of intense color across the whole mosaic.

FIX IT

198 **Avoid dull backgrounds**

If you have a plain background area to fill, you can avoid boring areas of flat color by mixing tiles or materials of different hues, such as the red and orange here.

TRY IT

197 **Make color drawings**

Using colored pencils on paper can be a good way to judge whether a color plan will work or not.

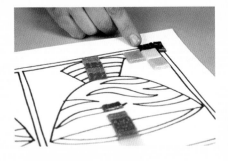

2 | Match colored pencils to the colors of the tiles selected, trying to make the matches as accurate as possible.

1 | Take your scaled-up drawing (see pages 78–79) and start to select a palette of tile colors. In this design the aim is to depict the bright, lively bowls as being in the foreground, setting them against a subtle background. It would be possible to contrast the foreground and background treatments by laying the bowls against a single color, but that would not create any tension between the two areas, and the bowls would be the only point of interest.

3 | Color in the drawing using the pencils, matching not only the colors but also their degrees of intensity. This can give you an idea of how well the design balances. If you feel your selection gives too much weight to one area of the composition, introduce another intense area to balance it.

199

Know the theory

A closer analysis of how color works is a useful exercise, so refer to the color wheel (below) to discover some of the important rules that govern the way colors work when placed together. Experiment with tiles from different positions within the color wheel to see the results for yourself.

200

Complementary colors

Colors on opposite sides of the wheel are known as "complementary colors," and when they are placed together they will seem almost to react with and separate from each other. When placed side by side, complementary colors make each other appear brighter.

The vibrancy that complementary colors can produce is used to great effect in this kingfisher. When the tone of complementary colors is very close, the reaction between them creates a shimmering effect.

201

Harmonious colors

The colors that are near to each other on the wheel are harmonious when placed together, tending to merge rather than clash.

Cool colors have an immediately cool and calming impact, often adding depth to a design.

Warm colors give a picture an energetic, busy, perhaps even unsettling feeling.

TRY IT

202
Make a choice
Using only warm or cool colors in a piece will give it a strongly atmospheric effect.

All warm   *All cool*

203

Color temperature

Colors can be classed as either warm or cool, and by using these effectively you can achieve a sense of space and distance between background and foreground. Cool colors tend to recede, while warm colors advance, therefore a warm-colored motif will stand out effectively against a background of cool colors. Generally, reds, oranges, and yellows are warm, and blues, violets, and greens are cool. A cool color is "warmed-up" if it contains traces of a warm color. For instance, a bluish-green is cooler than a yellowish-green.

Experiment with your tiles to see how using a contrasting background color can make a central motif stand out.

204

Create contrast

Contrast is the difference in the color and "brightness" of an object and its background, and can therefore be used to make elements of a picture stand out, or, conversely, blend together. Choosing colors with high contrast can help with the readability of the design, ensuring that the image is clear. Think about contrast when choosing the background color of a design.

205

Use color to create 3D effects

Using the tonal qualities of color is extremely effective in creating the impression of three-dimensionality. The shell motifs in this mosaic panel stand out in a clear and three-dimensional way from the background, because of the clever use of color.

If the contents of this bowl had not been surrounded by the lighter color of the bowl itself, the image would have been very unclear, because the tone of the contents and the tone of the tablecloth are very similar. It is the bright contrast of the bowl that makes the picture comprehensible.

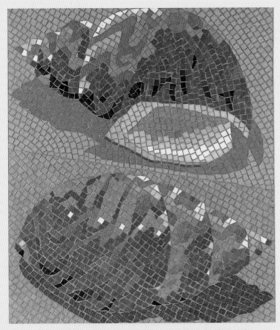

Light, mid, and dark tones gradate over the shells, giving them a rounded, and therefore three-dimensional, feel. The impression of three-dimensionality is heightened by the tonal variation of colors in the back- and foreground—a darker tone of each background color depicts each shell's shadow.

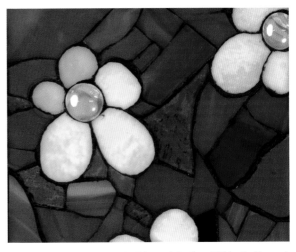

The intense color contrast in this work, Red and White by Taraneh Favagehi, beautifully enhances the simple design and makes a bold graphic statement.

Consider color: Grout

Grout is the great unknown, the one color not in your mosaic until the final phase. Your choice of grout color can enhance or complete your finished piece and unify the design. The wrong color can emphasize your mistakes and change your mosaic in undesirable ways.

FIX IT

206 **Midtones**
Many of the middle range of ceramic colors are similar in tone to the grout. This can, however, have the unfortunate effect of drawing midtones together and making strange united patches in what otherwise would be an evenly fractured mosaic. To overcome this problem, add a little lighter or a little darker grout to the gray mix, making a note of the proportions you mix.

207

Multiple grout tones

Of course you are not restricted to using a single grout color over your whole mosaic design, but can tailor your grouts to suit specific areas of your design. The grout in this example has been tailored to match tonally the different parts of the picture: light on the doves and dark on the background.

208

Choose grout colors carefully

Grout unites the surface of a mosaic, creating a connection between the colored tesserae, with varying consequences. With this in mind it is clear to see that your choice of grout color should be carefully considered. It takes a certain amount of experience to be able to foresee how the grout you use is going to affect the finished appearance of a mosaic, but to draw the image together, giving the mosaic a greater sense of unity and completeness, a good general rule is to grout the mosaic in the predominant tone of the piece.

There are several tonal options for grout. In the cooler range are white, gray, and black. For a warmer range there are pale yellows to dark brown. If you wish to unify your mosaic and the main tone is predominantly dark or bright, choose the darkest color of grout. If your mosaic is midrange in tone, use a unifying mid-gray tone, and for the lightest choose a pale tone.

209

White grout

White or light-colored grout complements light tones and especially well with broken ch (pique assiette) mosaics wher china is light to white in color. However, white grout can was the overall mosaic by drawing attention to the gaps rather th the tesserae themselves. Dark tesserae will appear isolated f each other, rather than unified Used on brighter, stronger col has a Mediterranean feel. Usir off-white or pale gray tone wil give a light feel, but make for "fractured" mosaic.

210

Mid-gray grout

Mid-gray grout provides an excellent neutral frame that shows off any color of tessera, except gray, of course. Gray often has the greatest unifying effect, treating both black and white equally. The brightest tesserae colors gain in brilliance and purity, softly glowing like jewels. Gray grout is a practical choice as well. If your mosaic is going to be walked on, whatever color grout you start with is inevitably going to end up gray.

211

Dark grout

Dark grout unifies dark-toned tesserae and isolates light ones. It increases the intensity of the tesserae colors so that they seem to glow.

White grout has a fracturing effect on the bright colors of these vitreous glass tiles, which are not light in tone. The high contrast between the grout and the tile colors fragments the arrangement.

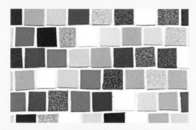

Here a ceramic mosaic panel has been grouted with white grout, illustrating the way the white grout draws attention to the paler colors of the piece.

The white grout in this marble mosaic panel brings out the intensity of the colors in the tiles. It emphasizes the lines which fractures the piece.

Mid-gray grout makes the vitreous glass tiles in this panel seem soft and subtle. Of all the samples, this one seems most to bring out the illusion of depth: some colors seem to recede, others to come closer.

Here the mid-toned grout brings out the mid-toned ceramic tiles. The range of colors in ceramic is fairly limited. If you are working in black and white, gray grout is usually the most sensible choice since it fractures both tones equally, rather than giving tonal precedence to one over the other.

Gray grout seems to give a softness to this marble mosaic panel and emphasizes the subtleties of the marbled surface.

Color depth and color brightness are sharply highlighted in this sample of vitreous glass and dark grout. The mid-gray of the previous glass sample and this grout unite the mid- and dark tones of the tiles in different ways.

Here, the darkest tones in the tiles are accentuated by the dark grout. Ceramic tiles can stain, so it is not advisable to leave dark grout smeared across them for any length of time.

Dark grout stresses a different set of tonal relationships to those you notice when the marble mosaic has been grouted in gray or white. Uniting the dark tones of the marble tiles intensifies the colors and creates an illusion of the lightest advancing and darkest tiles receding.

TRY IT

 212 **Coloring your own grout**

If you are looking for a different or more specific shade, or just want a small amount, you can color your own grout. Begin with either white or gray grout, depending on the final color you are after. Mix acrylic paint or powdered mineral-based colorants into your grout. If using acrylic paint the liquid will replace some of the water you would normally use to mix your grout to the proper consistency. Powdered colorants provide the best selection of colors, but a little goes a long way, you need to experiment with how much pigment to add.

When you color grout yourself, always make sure you make a generous quantity, because it is difficult to perfectly match a second batch.

213

Where can I find powdered colorants?

For the best selection of colors, research vendors who sell concrete colorants.

214

Decisions, decisions

When you have a number of grout colors in mind, to help the decision-making process try sprinkling different areas of the mosaic with a little dry grout in the colors under consideration. This gives you a good sense of what the final grout color will look like.

Test grout colors by sprinkling dry grout over your mosaic.

1 | Pour some paint into the grout. Because the grout is already white, any color you add will be weakened to a pastel shade; to make a dark tone or strong color you will need to add quite a lot of paint, or begin with gray grout.

2 | Mix thoroughly. To ensure that when you spread the grout it is of an even color consistency, you need to be sure there are no pockets of paint or colorant in the grout at this mixing stage. Follow slaking recommendations made by the manufacturer.

215

Taped-off areas

To grout in multiple colors, simply tape off the areas you do not want to be a certain color, grout the required areas, and leave to set. Once set, reverse the tape and grout your next color. Taping off areas will give you a strong, clean line as seen here in *Pear Tree* by Bonnie Fitzgerald.

216

Using multiple grout colors

Using more than one color of grout can enhance your finished mosaic in many ways. You can "punch up" your final work and create a high contrast between elements by using multiple colors.

When using multiple colors, you can "feather" the grout colors into each other, as seen in the center of the pansy.

Above: In Pansy, *Bonnie Fitzgerald uses different colored grout to unify the elements in different parts of the composition: the center of the flower was grouted purple, the petals were grouted yellow, and the leaves and foliage were grouted dark green.*

TRY IT

217 **Make sample panels**

There is no going back on grouting; you have to get it right first time. For this reason, do not hesitate to work up some sample panels with a selection of the tiles you have chosen for your design, and use these to experiment with differing grout colors.

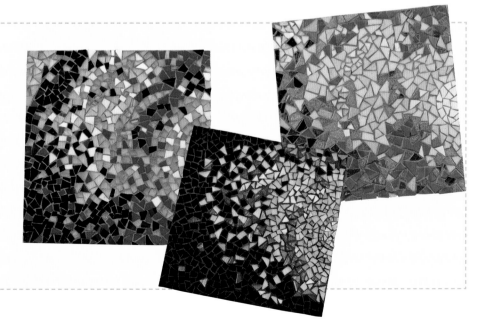

Color project: Red pepper

This project takes the form of a classic still life in which, like a painter, you learn to create a sense of light and shadow from solid raw materials. The bold coloring of the subject helps keep things simple—the piece uses just a few tones to create a luscious red pepper that looks good enough to eat.

13¹/₂in (34.5cm)

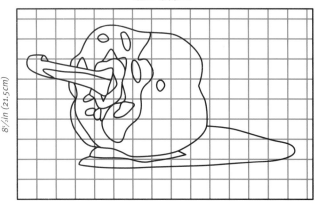

8¹/₂in (21.5cm)

Scale the design (see pages 78–79) and transfer it directly onto the substrate, following the technique described on page 115.

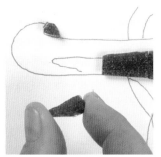

▲ **1 |** Begin with the darkest tone of the stalk, laying the dark green tiles. Use duller greens to give the fibrous, woody feel of the stalk.

Palette

White   Light red

Bottle green   Rose

Burgundy   Light green

Dark red   Mint Green

Ice blue

You will need

Vitreous glass tesserae

Pen

Wheel cutters or tile nippers

Adhesive and gluing tools

Grout and grouting tools

▲ **2 |** Around the base of the stalk, use some darker red tiles to give emphasis and strength.

◄ **3 |** Next, move on to the pink highlights to establish the left edge of the pepper. This is the lightest of the three reds you need in your color palette. Use rounded white tiles for the highlights.

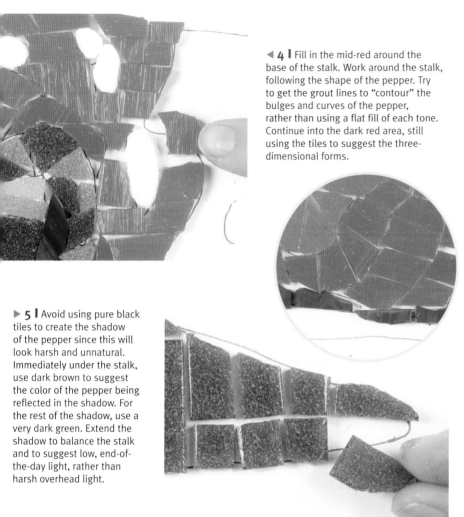

◄ **4** ❙ Fill in the mid-red around the base of the stalk. Work around the stalk, following the shape of the pepper. Try to get the grout lines to "contour" the bulges and curves of the pepper, rather than using a flat fill of each tone. Continue into the dark red area, still using the tiles to suggest the three-dimensional forms.

► **5** ❙ Avoid using pure black tiles to create the shadow of the pepper since this will look harsh and unnatural. Immediately under the stalk, use dark brown to suggest the color of the pepper being reflected in the shadow. For the rest of the shadow, use a very dark green. Extend the shadow to balance the stalk and to suggest low, end-of-the-day light, rather than harsh overhead light.

218

Complementary shading

The French Impressionists painted shadows with a hint of the color opposite to the object, a technique that can also be utilized in mosaic terms. The shadow of an object, most noticeably a strongly colored one, will contain a hint of the object's complementary color—in this case green as the opposite of the red of the pepper. By using strongly contrasting complementary colors that are tonally close together you can create realistic shadow effects.

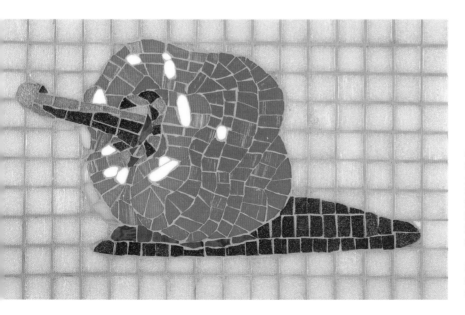

◄ The background is finished off with a simple opus regulatum pattern (see page 52) in a third strong color. Try to keep all the background tesserae whole—you'll need to master concave cuts so that the background fits the shape of the pepper.

To complete this exercise in using color, glue and grout, using the direct method (see pages 114–116).

Tessellations

A tessellation is a pattern that fits exactly together in a way that can be repeated indefinitely. Simple tessellations are made up of a single geometric shape such as a square or triangle; complex tessellations may combine a number of different shapes that interlock to form a repeat pattern.

Tessellations are one of the basic elements of mosaics, and have been used since ancient times. Simple tessellations of square tiles can provide interest and variation to backgrounds and borders. Even if you confine yourself to the simplest repeating patterns of square tiles, the variety you can produce just through different color choices is remarkable.

219

Start simple

The basic checkerboard is the simplest example of a tessellation. Square tiles in different colors are arranged in a rigid square grid, and this pattern can be used to add interest to flat areas of a design. Plan your grid carefully, to ensure it fits evenly into the area you need to cover—you do not want to end up with tiny slivers of tiles at one edge.

A variation of the checkerboard tessellation is to split alternate tiles in two. However, it isn't quite as easy as it looks—the split tiles need to be trimmed slightly to allow space for grout between them.

Uncut tiles in two colors make up this modest checkerboard tessellation.

If you don't trim the split tiles, the two halves will be wider than the tiles above and below and the pattern won't work.

JARGON BUSTER ◆
TESSELLATE
A repeat pattern without gaps or overlapping.

FIX IT

220 **Use with caution**
Complex tessellations are strong designs that are best rendered simply and boldly in their own right. Using anything but the simplest of tessellations within other designs risks introducing a distracting and likely overpowering element.

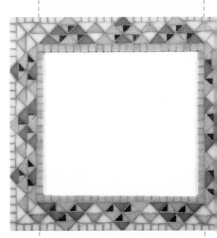

This complex pyramid tessellation is striking in its own right, and should not be combined with another design. Instead use a pattern like this as a mirror frame or decorative border on a wall.

221 Cut it up

Create more complex patterns by cutting tiles in the usual ways.

Here, a zigzag tessellation has been created using quarter-cut tiles of different colors. Using smaller tiles like this is an ideal way to make interesting borders or frames for your designs.

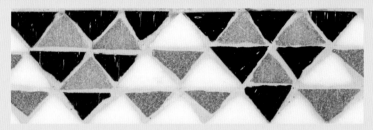

Here, small triangles have been cut and arranged in a simple repeat, with a double tessellation created through the use of color, so that the larger blocks of nine tiles form a second repeat of triangles. The alternating blocks are also "positive" and "negative" versions of each other.

This design works on a very simple grid of squares, but with each square filled with two diagonally cut tiles with colors alternated to give a diamond pattern.

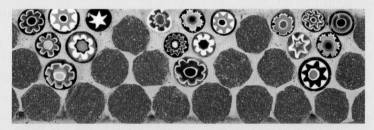

A triangular pattern has been repeated using circular-cut tiles and millefiori. While not strictly a tessellation, the repeat of circular tiles can provide a looser "bubbly" effect that will suit some designs.

222 Ancient inspiration

Many striking ancient mosaics, such as this one from Corinth in Greece, use tessellations of geometric and interlocking shapes, and could inspire your own tessellation designs.

TRY IT

223 Prepare a grid

For many tessellations, the grid consists of basic squares repeated over and over, and it can be difficult to remember your color pattern: if you get one tile wrong the whole pattern falls to pieces. Make a grid plan on paper and shade in the squares of the grid for the different colors you are using, so that you don't get confused and make mistakes when you start to glue the tiles down.

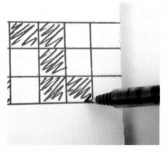

Plan your pattern on paper to avoid making mistakes when laying your tesserae.

224

Designing a repeat fan tessellation

This fan tessellation may look complicated, but it is actually a relatively easy pattern to produce, since it does not require too much complex cutting.

1 I To begin planning the way your fans will tessellate, first draw a circle. Put the point of a drawing compass on any point on the edge of the circle and draw another. Where these two circles cross, place the point of the compass and draw another one. Continue until there are interrelated shapes across the sheet of paper. The paper is now covered with fan shapes. Select the orientation of the fans from the three obvious choices: all fans laid pointing to the right; all laid pointing to the left; or they alternate. This design takes the alternating option. Mark your choice on your sketch.

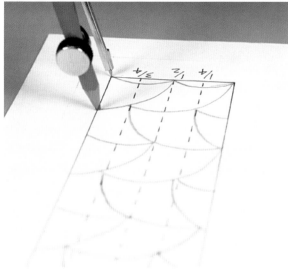

2 I Decide how many repeats you want, based on the area you wish to cover and the size of the tile module. Produce a scaled-down drawing of your work, divide it into four sections, and draw guidelines from the top to the bottom. These guidelines let you check if the points of the fans line up accurately. It is surprisingly easy for little inaccuracies to occur, and small inaccuracies become much larger over a substantial area. Start from the bottom corner of the design.

3 I Make a template of one fan to the size you require and draw around this to create the entire design. If you are working directly (see pages 114–116) you can transfer the design to your substrate. If working indirectly (see pages 124–129), as here, transfer the design to brown paper.

4 I Begin applying the tiles to the substrate or paper. You may want to lay the tiles in place before gluing in order to judge your use of color. Although this design does not require a great deal of cutting, there are areas where the cutting is critical, especially along the edges of the fans. Cut the angled tiles first, then lay tiles into the center. You may have to trim central tiles to ensure an even fit, however, if you need to trim tiles for several lines in succession, make sure that the edges of cut tiles do not line up with one another.

Gold-leaf tiles are expensive, but they give an intense effect, so you can cut a number of very small tiles from each one.

This design uses a random mix of colors, but you could emphasize the shapes by using gradated tones within each fan.

Tessellation project: Swimming fish

To achieve the effect of a fish swimming serenely in an ornamental pond, both the body of the fish and the fan-filled background need to be rendered as smoothly as possible. The black tiles in particular must be cut to give a smooth outline to the fish's markings, avoiding any jagged mismatch of neighboring tiles.

8½in (21cm)

12in (30cm)

Scale or copy the design (see page 78–79) and transfer it directly onto the substrate, following the technique described on page 115. Follow the technique described on pages 104–105 to mark in the fan-tessellation background.

Palette

Pale Green	Ice blue
Sky blue	Bright white
Blood orange	Black

You will need

Vitreous glass tesserae

Millefiori bead

Pen

Grease pencil (optional)

Wheel cutters or tile nippers

Adhesive and gluing tools

Grout and grouting tools

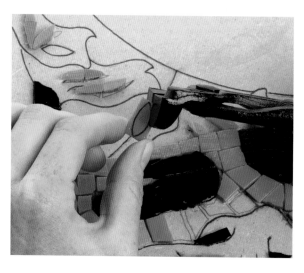

◄ **1 |** Place the black and orange tiles of the fish first, using a pen or grease pencil to accurately mark your cuts. Cut the orange tiles in half, then taper the ends to a point to mimic the distinctive markings of the fins and tail. The rounded D-shaped tiles are crucial to achieving the flowing outline and curves of the mouth and the black and orange markings on the body of the fish.

▶ **2 |** The hook-shaped points at the ends of the fins and tail are equally important. Carefully mark the tiles to accurately follow the drawing.

225

Glue as you go

It is tempting to layout entire projects without committing to gluing them in place. When using small tesserae, once you dry lay a small area and are happy, stick it. It is easy to accidentally move your substrate or lose all of your work with a sneeze, so get the adhesive out before this happens.

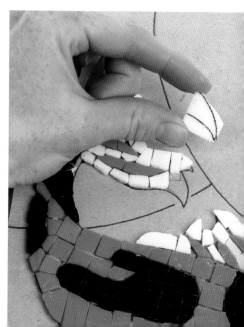

◄ **3 ▮** Precut lots of quarter-tiles for the background. Follow the fan layout carefully, but mix the colors in a random way.

▼ **4 ▮** Use a carefully selected millefiori bead for the eye of the fish.

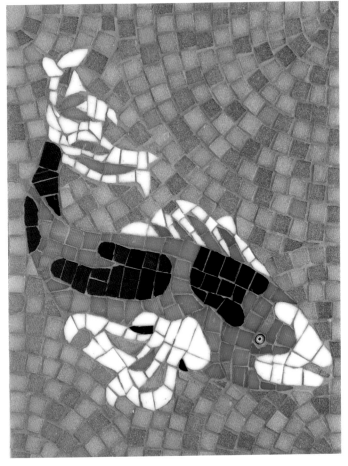

▶ **5 ▮** Complete this exercise in using a fan tessellation by gluing with white craft glue and grouting, using the direct method (see pages 114–116).

The fan shapes suggest ripples on the water and create a sense of movement. The color palette for the fish is much stronger than the water, which makes the fish stand out even more.

Templates: Patterns

If you are unsure how to structure your mosaic visually, consider taking a leaf out of the Romans' book and use medallions or motifs on a simple background, surrounded by a basic or intricate border. In fact, there are many traditional sources you can draw on and make your own, perhaps historical, in nature, or with a nod to the world of art.

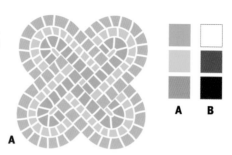

A

A   B

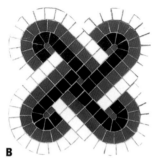

B

226

Guilloche knot ◄

This motif has a Celtic look, although it is based on a Roman design. The color combination retains a traditional feel, but the motif works equally well when given a modern spin by using citrus colors.

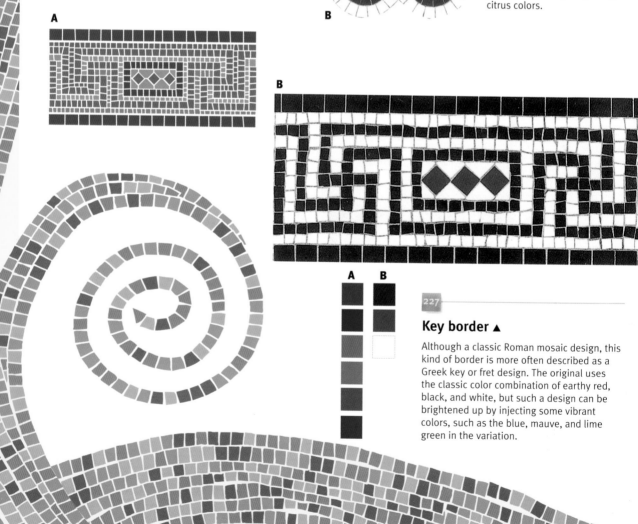

A

B

A   B

227

Key border ▲

Although a classic Roman mosaic design, this kind of border is more often described as a Greek key or fret design. The original uses the classic color combination of earthy red, black, and white, but such a design can be brightened up by injecting some vibrant colors, such as the blue, mauve, and lime green in the variation.

228

Leafy border ▶

Images from the natural world can be used to build up patterns, as in this leafy border mosaic. The leaves are set at lively angles against a regular background, and the berries, set at intervals and with their bright hue, increase the interest. The variation experiments with increasing the tonal differences in the pattern, particularly between the leaves and the background.

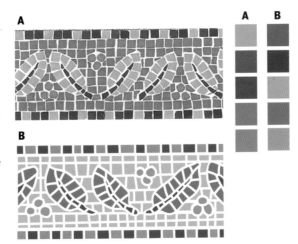

231

Give your eyes a helping hand

When working on a pattern with many intersecting lines that cross over in a very deliberate way it may be easiest to outline it first so your eyes don't fool you. In *Celtic Knot*, made using viterous glass tesserae by Kenneth Fitzgerald, the right side of the ribbon always crosses over the previous swirl.

229

Triangle border ◀

Using whole mosaic tiles means this border is one of the easiest to make. Its abstract nature also makes it a good choice when mixing lots of different colors. The original uses classic colors—ocher, black, and white—but a jazzy version could contrast acid yellow and pink with warm terracotta and dense black and purple.

230

Twist border ▶

This simple but effective twist makes a lively border. It looks especially good on a floor, or on any mosaic that covers a large enough space to feature a number of twist motifs. You can choose to execute this design using a dark twist on a light background, such as the brown against cream used here, or consider a light twist on a dark background, as in the color variation, which features a light green twist on a darker blue background.

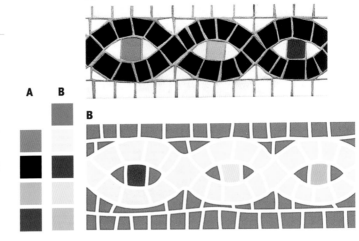

Templates: The everyday— past and present

One of the best aspects of the mosaic art is the sheer breadth of scope it offers the creative mind, and almost anything can provide inspiration. Just as earlier cultures put the things that were important in their lives into their mosaics, we are doing the same.

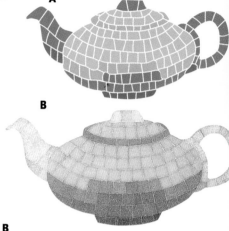

A

B

232

Vintage motorbike ▼

Reproducing this vintage motorbike is not for the faint-hearted mosaicist, since many of the tesserae are individually shaped; nevertheless it is a very satisfying achievement. This mosaic has been built up in colors that approximate to the real thing, but there is no reason not to try some bolder colors, such as the reds demonstrated in the variation.

A   B

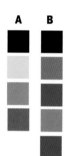

233

Teapot ▲

Immortalized in this mosaic is a much-used and loved teapot that was treasured for its beautiful shape, but eventually broke through pure wear and tear. The gentle curves of the andamento caress its shape, and the soft gradation of several tones give the effect of filling out the rounded body. Alternative adaptations should take care to reproduce the curves in the same way, as does this color variation in shades of warm green.

A   B

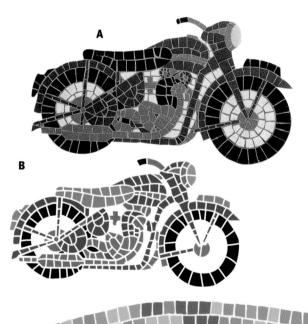

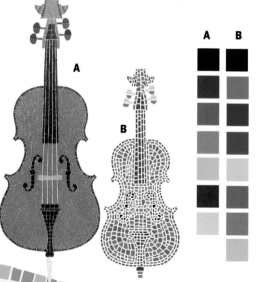

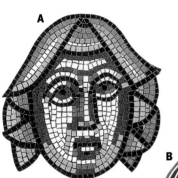

A

A

Geometric flower ▼

The strong colors used in this motif are successfully distributed over a pale background, the whole being bound together by the dark border. The variation uses dark blue instead of black for the border, and employs some fairly colorful hues as a change from the earthy colors of the original.

B

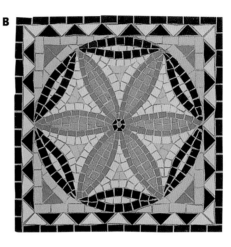

B

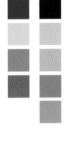

A   B

234

Man's head ▲

There is a medieval air about this head mosaic. Although the design does not attempt to imitate a realistic face, it is expressive nonetheless. The bold outline is important and is therefore retained in the alternative version, as is the way the face is broken up into blocks of color. This overall style does not suit a naturalistic approach, or an overcomplicated or modern color palette.

A   B

237

Greek boat ▼

This boat mosaic has the ring of a traditional style of Greek art. The limited palette of earthy colors reinforces this effect. The tesserae on the boat flow horizontally to echo its shape; but within the rectangular frame of the sail, they work diagonally, facilitating the thin crisscross pattern. The variation also avoids too diverse a palette, leaving the viewer to focus on the design.

A

236

Cello ◄

In this mosaic the lines of tesserae beautifully complement the cello's curved form, and the strings are indicated by the gaps between the tesserae. These interstices are wider than in the rest of the mosaic to make a feature of the strings. Carefully cut wedge-shaped pieces of tesserae form a beautiful curve that perfectly resembles the body of the instrument. The coloring is rich but simple; the tesserae are black or midtoned, while the grout is pale, creating a well-balanced and, in the original, very realistic piece. In the variation, shades of blue are graded across the body of the instrument.

B

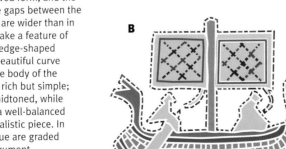

A   B

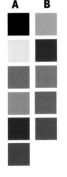

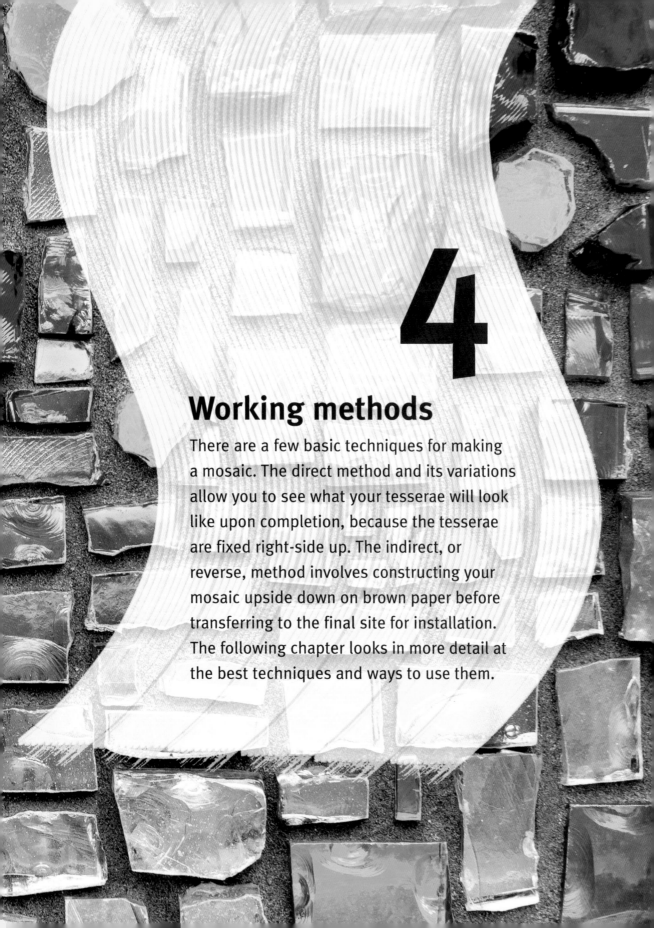

4

Working methods

There are a few basic techniques for making a mosaic. The direct method and its variations allow you to see what your tesserae will look like upon completion, because the tesserae are fixed right-side up. The indirect, or reverse, method involves constructing your mosaic upside down on brown paper before transferring to the final site for installation. The following chapter looks in more detail at the best techniques and ways to use them.

Direct techniques

The direct method is a good technique for beginners to use because it is relatively quick and easy. The tesserae are fixed directly onto the substrate right-side up. This method's biggest advantage is that what you see while you are working is very close in appearance to the finished product.

Why work directly?

The direct method has the advantage of being immediate—you can see the results as you work—unlike the reverse method, which requires you to work back-to-front (see pages 124–129). However, the direct method is only possible for artworks created in your studio or where the location is suitable and allows you time to complete the piece. Large mosaics or those to be sited outside are best constructed indirectly before being transferred to their final sites.

- Working directly means you can see exactly what the mosaic will look like as you progress.
- The direct method allows you to see the true colors and shapes of the tesserae as you work.
- Working directly gives you more control over gradations in color because the face sides of the tesserae are visible.
- The direct method can be used when a perfectly flat surface is not important.
- Use the direct method if your tesserae are not of a uniform depth, shape, or size and you want to make use of that surface irregularity/texture.
- Tesserae must be laid directly if your substrate is sculpted or concave.

JARGON BUSTER ◆ DRY LAY

The term used to describe the process of laying tesserae in place without adhesive, for planning purposes.

Working directly onto the surface

The direct method is so called because you glue the cut tesserae directly onto your substrate.

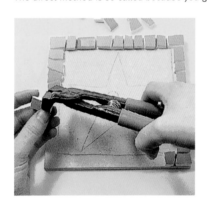 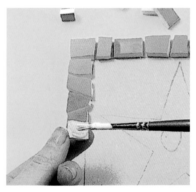 

1 I Prepare your substrate so that it is ready to install (see Plan ahead, page 20), and prime the surface as necessary (see Prepare MDF, page 20), before directly transferring your design to the substrate. Working on a small area at a time—here the border is planned first—cut and place tiles right side up and without glue. Move and rearrange pieces until they are just right, and don't be afraid to discard a piece that doesn't fit or has imperfections. Remember to leave gaps between the tesserae for grouting (see Leave gaps for grout, page 58).

2 I When you are happy with the first area, move the pieces to one side, keeping them in formation. Use a spatula to spread glue over a part of the planned area, remembering to take into consideration the adhesive's drying time, and so only covering an area you can complete in that time. For detailed pieces, use a fine paintbrush to dab glue onto the bottom of the tesserae.

3 I Follow Steps 1–2 to continue placing and gluing tesserae in the other areas of the design, and when complete leave the mosaic for 24 hours to dry thoroughly before grouting.

240
Direct transferring

It is far easier to work accurately to your design if it is drawn onto your substrate. There are a few ways to do this. You can place transfer or carbon paper face down on your substrate, tape your pattern on top, and carefully trace the pattern. A less expensive approach is to use tracing paper to make your own carbon paper.

1 | First copy your pattern onto tracing paper. Turn the tracing over and trace over the back of the design with soft pencil.

2 | Turn the tracing the right-side up and place it in the correct position on your substrate. You will find the transferring process easier if you tape the paper onto the surface. Using a hard, sharp pencil, retrace the outline of the drawing. The pencil line that you have just made on the back of the drawing will act like carbon paper, transferring the design onto the substrate.

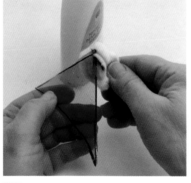

3 | Carefully pull back the tracing from one corner to check that you have gone over all the lines, and lay it back if you need to redo any missed areas. When you are happy, remove the paper completely and go over any faint lines on the substrate to ensure you can clearly see the design.

241
Keep it light

Using a marker pen to draw your design onto your substrate may make it difficult to make drawing corrections if you are using clear or translucent tesserae, because marks will probably show through. Use a light pencil in those instances.

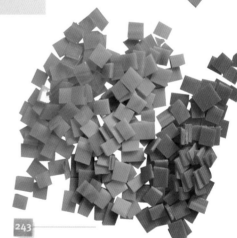

242
Glass on glass

When you are working with stained glass you can draw your pattern with a felt tip pen directly onto the glass and remove the line later with nail polish remover. Alternatively, you can also tape your pattern to the back of your glass as shown in the Glass on glass project (see pages 142–143).

243
Your tesserae pool

Having a pool of ready-cut tesserae will help the laying down process go faster. If you are using tesserae of a generally similar size, create a pool of precut materials, but do not cut everything at once. Instead, aim to cut half of what you think you will need. This will leave you with materials for special cuts, and save on wastage.

244

How to work directly with uneven tiles and still achieve a flat surface

Working directly with found materials—such as broken tiles—is challenging because the materials will not necessarily be all of the same thickness. However, it is possible to build up the backs of the tiles with cement-based adhesive or mastic to produce a flat, practical surface. This is called building up your setting bed.

1 I Begin by laying the area of your design that uses the thickest tiles. All the tiles need to be laid to the depth of the thickest tile in order to be perfectly flat, so by starting with these elements you will establish a target height for all the other tiles. Apply thinset or mastic with a spatula or small tool.

2 I Check that the mosaic has been laid flat before the adhesive has set. To do this, use a light hammer and a small board, gently tapping the area you have laid to ensure the surface is level. If the adhesive has already set, you risk breaking the bond. If adhesive squeezes up between the joints as you tap, scrape it away with a knife. If you find that some tiles are low, take them out and build up the level with more adhesive.

3 I Once the thickest tiles have been laid, you can begin work on other areas. Again, the order of your work depends on the thickness of the tiles. Place progressively thicker layers of adhesive under the thinner tiles, and continue to check for flatness using a hammer and board, as in Step 2.

245

Many and varied materials

Working with a wide variety of tiles and materials can make for beautiful surface enhancements. These door stoops and lamp post were created using 30 different glass and ceramic tiles, and beautifully unify the landscape. Each individual tessera required seating by back buttering, but the effort was well worth it.

Double direct techniques

The two versions of the double direct method of mosaic making involve using face tape or fiberglass mesh. Both allow you to see the face of your tesserae, so you will have a good idea of what the finished piece will look like. Also, both methods make for easy storage and transport of your mosaic.

TRY IT

246 **Packing tape**
A cost-effective alternative to face tape is clear packing tape, which works fine as long as your tesserae are not too heavy.

247 Face taping small projects

If you have dry laid your design and are happy with it, you can save yourself the work of removing and gluing each individual tessera by using face tape. Another advantage of this method is that even if you use tiles of different thicknesses the finished piece will have a relatively flat surface. This method is not recommended for large works, since the tesserae are likely to move around as you lay on the tape.

1 I When you are happy with your dry-laid mosaic, cut a piece of face tape to the size of your design. Lay the sticky side on the face of the tesserae, taking care not to disturb them, because once they have adhered to the plastic you cannot change their positions easily.

2 I Sandwich the mosaic between two boards and turn it over.

3 I Apply adhesive to the surface the mosaic is to be sited on. Place the mosaic in position over the adhesive, with the plastic side up. With a small board and hammer tap the mosaic flat to ensure even the smallest piece has made contact with the adhesive.

4 I Give the adhesive time to dry before peeling away the tape. Finish by grouting in the usual way.

248 Why choose double direct with face tape?

Working double direct with face tape enables you to create an easily transportable mosaic in a controlled environment: on a flat surface, temperature controlled, and with all of your materials and tools close at hand.
• Using face tape is a great way to temporarily preserve your work. Work surfaces shift and tables get bumped, but if the mosaic is face taped in place it is protected.
• This is a good technique for large exterior works to be sited in flat areas. The mosaic can be cut into manageable sections and easily transported.
• Use face tape for mosaics that will be sited underwater, because—unlike when using mesh—there is nothing between the back of the tesserae and the installation surface. You seat the mosaic directly into the bed of adhesive on site, guaranteeing no water will get behind the tesserae and compromise the installation.
• Be advised that this method does not work well with smalti, or if your tesserae are of various thicknesses.

FIX IT

249 **Clean up**
The face tape may not stick if your tesserae are dirty, so it is a good idea to wash your tesserae before you begin and to keep your work surface clear.

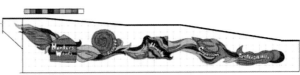

250

Face taping a large project

Large-scale projects are not for the faint of heart. Do not underestimate the amount of preparation work for large-scale works. Success depends on careful planning and lots of helping hands. This project at Hunters Woods Elementary School, in Reston, Virginia, was done with the help of 200 youth and parent volunteers.

1 I Make a pattern to fit the final installation site. One way of doing this is to scan the design into a computer program and digitally place it in on the site. Above, each grid square represents one square foot. When you are happy with the design, create a full-size black and white pattern on which to build the mosaic.

2 I Tape your pattern onto a flat surface and place clear contact paper, sticky side up, over the top (this serves as a temporary adhesive). Position your tesserae, right side up, on the contact paper using the pattern beneath to guide you.

3 I When the whole mosaic is complete, apply face tape over the surface of the design, taking care not to disturb the tiles. You will need to overlap the face tape to join pieces together (see Overlap edges, above). The face tape must be stronger that the contact paper.

   The mosaic will need to be cut into manageable sections for transportation to the installation site. Take lots of photos of the complete mosaic, then mark where you will cut the mosaic, along with registration marks, so you can easily reassemble them on location. Cut the mosaic into pieces by slicing through the face tape with a box cutter or an X-acto knife.

4 I Transport the mosaic to the job site on boards with the contact paper intact. Dry lay the mosaic near the installation site so that you can assemble it in order.

FIX IT

251 **Overlap edges**
Face tape is usually purchased in 6 or 12in (15 or 30cm) rolls, or 12in (30cm) squares. If you need to use more than one piece of tape on a large project, be sure to overlap the edges by at least ½in (1cm).

JARGON BUSTER ◆ REGISTRATION MARKS
A mark (a letter, number, or symbol) made on each side of a mosaic before it is cut and used to reassemble the mosaic by matching the marks together.

5 I Place the pattern on the wall and outline it with chalk. Apply a "scratch coat" to the site—a very thin layer of the same thinset that will be used to adhere the mosaic to the wall. This smooths out the installation surface (filling mortar lines in the brickwork, for example) and will help create a "mechanical bond" between the new thinset, the mosaic, and the wall.

6 I Apply adhesive to the scratch coat in manageable sections to match those of the cut face-taped mosaic. Remove the contact paper from these sections and seat them into the adhesive. Work methodically from one side to the next. Match your registration marks exactly before setting the entire puzzle piece into the adhesive—this way you can get a tight fit.

8 I Seeing your finished mosaic installed at its final location is bittersweet because unless it is in your home you will no longer have the artwork in your life everyday. But as a public work of art, sharing your work with others has its own reward.

7 I Allow the adhesive to dry, peel the face tape off, then grout. Grouting on a large work can take several hours, so only mix what you can handle in the time you have available. When working on location protect areas you do not want grout to stain by covering them with plastic sheets.

FIX IT

252 **Pop it back in**
If a piece of tesserae falls out during installation, simply butter the back (see page 24) and push it back into place.

253

Vertical installation

When installing on a wall, if possible start with a bottom lower corner, and work section by section, pressing the mosaic into place. If necessary, place a board or other straight object below the first row of sections to keep them from slipping down the wall. Sometimes this isn't possible, so try using masking or painters tape to hold the sections in place until they set. Stretch a piece of tape from the center of the mosaic section up and onto the wall area above it. Do this in a couple of places.

Masking tape has been used to hold the vertical sections of mosaic in place while they set.

254

Why choose double direct on mesh?

Double direct on mesh is a common technique used for architectural applications such as backsplashes. It is also an efficient way to create large-format and/or complex designs, transport them easily, and preserve your work.

- Work on mesh if the size of the artwork makes it difficult or impossible to create it on-site.
- For very large works the mesh—with the mosaic already fixed to it—can be cut into sections for ease of transportation and installation.
- The mosaic on the mesh can be easily stored and is straightforward to install.
- Mesh is flexible, so if your final application is curved, such as a column, mesh mounting is the best fabrication method.
- Creating a mosaic on a vertical surface can be difficult because the tesserae may slide down before the adhesive cures. An easier way is to fabricate the design on a sheet of fiberglass mesh and glue the entire sheet of mosaic to the wall. This allows you to work on a horizontal surface and create detailed designs that would otherwise be impossible.

256

What is mesh?

Mesh is made with fiberglass in a crosshatched manner, which allows the final mounting adhesive to push through the mesh and "grab" the tesserae along the sides and bottom. You can purchase it from specialty mosaic stores. Be sure to buy alkali-resistant mesh if you are using thinset as your adhesive.

255

Double direct on mesh technique

PVA glue is a temporary adhesive used to fix the tesserae to the mesh. The adhesive you use to mount the finished mosaic to its substrate is the final and permanent adhesive.

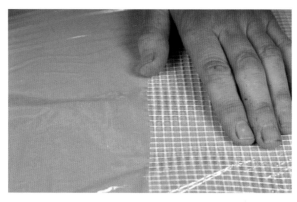

1 I Make a pattern by directly transferring your scaled-up design. Cut the mesh to size and sandwich a piece of plastic between your pattern and the mesh, to ensure you don't glue the tesserae to the pattern.

2 I Either apply PVA glue to each individual tile or, as shown here, apply a line of glue directly to the mesh and set each tile. It is not necessary for the entire back of the piece to be covered in glue for it to adhere to the mesh.

When the mosaic is complete, leave to dry overnight. The next day you can peel the plastic sheeting off the back to allow the mosaic to finish drying.

3 I When you are ready to install, mix up the correct amount of the appropriate adhesive, in this example thinset.

FIX IT

257 **Use as little PVA glue as possible**
Too much PVA glue will prevent the thinset or mastic from fully "grabbing" the tesserae through the mesh.

4 I Apply adhesive to the surface the mosaic is to be sited on. Remember it is the thinset that bonds the tessarae to the substrate.

FIX IT

258 **Clean your grout lines**
If using thinset to install the mosaic, you may find excess adhesive squeezing up in between the tesserae. Be sure to clean the grout lines while the thinset is still wet. Cocktail sticks or a flat-head screwdriver may prove easy tools for this job, or use your stir stick.

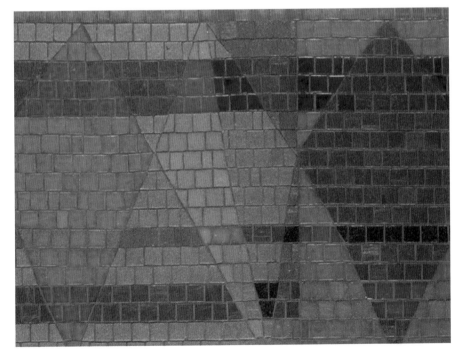

5 I Carefully align one corner of the mosaic with the corner of your substrate and place the mosaic into the adhesive. To be sure each piece of tesserae has enough adhesive on the back, and that the mosaic will be flat, take a hammer and small board and gently tap the entire surface.

6 I Allow the adhesive to cure, then grout in the color of your choice.

This large wall mosaic was well suited to the double direct on mesh method of working. The artist could see exactly how to achieve the subtle color variations with detailed cutting.

259

Keen to proceed?

If you are in a hurry and need the mosaic on the mesh to dry quickly, once you have removed the plastic sheeting, gently turn the mosaic upside down and allow the air to reach the PVA glue directly. You can speed things up even further by using a hair dryer to dry the glue. However, you cannot use a hair dryer to speed up the drying of thinset—it needs to cure over time or it may weaken.

Direct working project: Flower

The flowing organic form of the flower in this direct method project is hugged closely by the curving, soft background. Look carefully at the photograph of the finished piece to see how two sides of the glass tiles are cut to create even curves. The petals are given emphasis by tiles cut in a hooked shape to give the rows more of an arch. This is a good example of opus musivum (see page 54).

11¹/₂ in (29 cm)

8¹/₄ in (21 cm)

Scale the design (see page 78–79) and transfer it directly onto the substrate, following the technique described on page 115.

Palette

Ice blue   *Rose*

Tangerine   *Dark red*

Khaki   *Putty*

Palest pink

You will need

Vitreous glass tesserae

Prepared baseboard

Pen

Wheel cutters or tile nippers

Adhesive and gluing tools

Grout and grouting tools

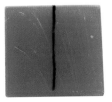 

▲ **1** ❙ Cut the flower center by cutting a tile in half and tapering the edge into a teardrop shape from each side. Cut all of these pendant shapes in advance, so that you can try different combinations to balance any slight discrepancy in their individual sizes before gluing them down.

◀ **2** ❙ Each putty-colored petal is cut from two whole tiles that are mirror images of each other.

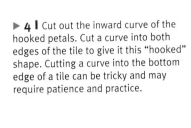

▶ **4 |** Cut out the inward curve of the hooked petals. Cut a curve into both edges of the tile to give it this "hooked" shape. Cutting a curve into the bottom edge of a tile can be tricky and may require patience and practice.

▲ **3 |** To make these small circles, first cut your tiles into quarters, then carefully cut away at the shape in a spiral until you have a circle.

◀ **5 |** Cut along tapered lines to make these fan-shaped pieces for the two outer rows of petals. When the whole of the flower motif is planned and you are happy with the way the tesserae fit together, begin gluing. Working on a small area at a time, move the tesserae to the side, but still in their places, and apply glue to the substrate—or bottom of the tesserae in detailed areas. Replace the tesserae elements before the glue dries.

▲ **6 |** For the background, cut a stock of quarter-tiles and then glue a ring that carefully follows the outline of the design. Add additional rings, working outward until the background is completely covered.

▶ When the glue is dry, grout in the usual way (see page 30). Gray grout has been used here to complete the mosaic.

Indirect reverse techniques

This indirect method is also known as the reverse method, because the image is reversed and you work on the back of the mosaic. It is indirect because you are not working on your final substrate or on the job site. With this technique the mosaic is constructed the "wrong" way round—with the tesserae backs facing you—on paper, and not directly onto its final substrate. The paper is a temporary surface and the mosaic is fixed right side up when it is finally positioned in this permanent location. It is the method most commonly used for floors and utilitarian surfaces such as table tops.

Why work indirectly in reverse?

The main advantages of working indirectly is that the mosaic can be made away from the installation site, in the comfort and controlled environment of your studio, and be easily stored and transported.

- When you work indirectly, your tesserae will lay flat, even if they are of different thicknesses.
- This method of working is ideal for table tops and floors because the final, grouted surface will be flat.

- As with double direct methods, this method allows you to complete the work in the comfort of your own workspace, then transport the mosaic to its final site at a convenient time.
- If necessary, you can continue to make changes to your mosaic right up until the day before final installation. If you are unhappy with an area, dampen the paper and remove the tesserae you wish to change.

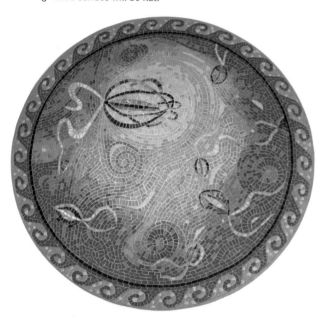

Left: This jellyfish floor medallion needed a flat, safe, slip-free surface. Artist Marian Shapiro constructed it using the reverse method, then cut it into sections for delivery and installation. The clients had preprepared the space in the floor—new floorboards had been laid and the edges lined with a brass ring.

FIX IT

261 Know where you are when working big

When working on a large indirect mosaic, it can be useful to divide the work up into manageable sections, since very large mosaics can be heavy and unwieldy when the tiles are on the paper. With the reversed design already on the brown paper, work out the best way to divide the large area into smaller sections, noting on your original drawing how you have made the divisions and allocating each section a code—such as A, B, C, D, etc.

It is also a good idea to take photographs, which can prove invaluable when you are reassembling your artwork.

1 I Once the design has been drawn on the paper, decide how you wish to divide up the mosaic into workable areas, keeping in mind the way in which the mosaic will finally be placed in position. Draw your section lines and mark your repositioning code on the original drawing, then cut out your brown paper section.

2 I Mark the section codes on the back of the relevant sheets of brown paper. Include directional arrows, because once the mosaic is covered with thinset or grout it may not be obvious which way is up.

262

Reverse your design

There are times when it is necessary to reverse your design drawing. The easiest way to do this is to trace your scaled-up design (see page 78–79)—or even scale-up your original design directly onto tracing paper—and turn the tracing over to transfer the motif to the brown paper that the tiles will be temporarily adhered to.

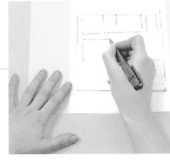

1 I Trace the design onto a sheet of tracing paper using a black marker pen. Do not turn the tracing paper over yet, but rub the pen lines with a soft lead pencil.

2 I Turn the tracing paper over and transfer the design onto the matte side of the brown paper by tracing over the black lines with a hard lead pencil. The design will now be in reverse.

263

Pre-grout

The technique of pre-grouting involves applying grout to the mosaic once it has adhered to its temporary paper backing, before it is embedded in its final adhesive. Carefully grouting at this stage prevents the final adhesive from coming up between the joints, and improves the adhesion of the mosaic to the backing material. It also begins to dampen the water-soluble glue used to temporarily fix the tiles to the paper, making the paper easier to remove. When the paper has been peeled away, the excess grout on the face of the mosaic must be sponged off while it is still wet, otherwise it will harden into an uneven surface.

1 I Once you have adhered your tiles to the paper (see Working indirectly on paper, pages 126–127), and the glue has had time to dry, apply the grout to the back of the tiles with a grouting squeegee or notched grout spreader. Make sure all the joints are filled. This is most easily achieved by sweeping the squeegee horizontally and then vertically.

2 I Wet your sponge and squeeze it out as much as possible. Clean off the excess grout by pressing one side of the sponge flat to the mosaic. Turn the sponge over and repeat. It is essential to use a clean area of sponge each time: otherwise you will simply reapply all the grout you previously removed. Make sure there is no grout left on the surface of the tiles, since this will prevent proper bonding with the adhesive on the final substrate. This is one of the rare times you may need to dampen your sponge during the grout process.

264

Working indirectly on paper

Brown parcel paper is strong and stable, and will soak up water when the time comes to remove it from the tiles. The glue used to fix the tiles to the paper needs to be water-soluble. In this example, water-soluble PVA glue diluted with water (one part glue to one part water) has been used, but you can also use a weak solution of wallpaper paste or flour paste. Flour paste is a mixture of flour and water heated until thick and is most often the adhesive of choice for professional artists working in this technique. Here we are working in vitreous glass tiles, which are flat on the front side and beveled on the back.

1 | Cut and arrange the tiles, wrong side up, using your reversed drawing as a guide. When you are happy with the arrangement, dilute PVA glue 50:50 with water and, working on small areas at a time, glue the tessarae in place, using a brush to apply the glue to the paper.

2 | When all tiles are glued down, leave to dry overnight, then pre-grout (see page 125).

3 | Use a notched grout spreader or trowel to apply a thinset adhesive to the substrate, aiming for an even coverage.

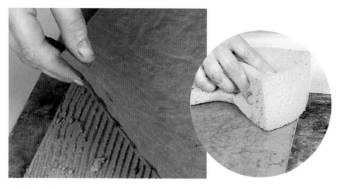

4 | Place the pre-grouted mosaic into the adhesive, paper side up. Be sure to align the corners properly before putting the paper in place.

5 | Wet the paper with a thoroughly wet sponge. Leave the paper to absorb moisture for at least five to ten minutes.

6 | Starting from one corner and working toward the center, peel back the paper. The tiles along the edge of the mosaic are the most vulnerable. If any come away, place them back in position. Once you have peeled into the center, start to peel from the opposing corner. Once the paper has been peeled off, clean the mosaic immediately with a thoroughly squeezed out sponge. Leave to dry.

7 | Once the mosaic is dry, re-grout it from the front (see page 30), making sure that all the tiny holes are filled. Wet a clean sponge and squeeze out as much water as possible. Use this to clean the grout off the mosaic and buff up with a soft cloth.

TRY IT

265 **Gummed paper**
Instead of applying glue to brown parcel paper when working indirectly, try using gummed brown paper, manufactured for general craft applications. Simply stick the tesserae face down onto the paper by wetting the paper or the surface of the tile with a paintbrush. Pre-grout and fix the mosaic to its final surface in the usual way.

The finished piece has a smooth surface, as a result of using the indirect reverse method. It was assembled in comfort at a workbench before being fixed into its final site.

266

How to work indirectly with marble: the double reverse method

The unfinished, sawn face of polished marble is dull, and its muted tones do not demonstrate the lively color of the finished side. When using these tiles you need to lay the design as if working directly, but bed it into a cement-based adhesive to level out any unevenness, which is why the double reverse method is a good choice. Although marble tesserae will not be uniform, they do need to be roughly the same thickness, since working in this way is slightly trickier than simply working in reverse.

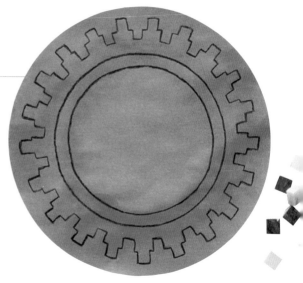

1 I Directly transfer (see page 115) your design onto a piece of brown paper, and cut to the size and shape of the finished project. Cut another sheet of brown paper the same size and shape as the first.

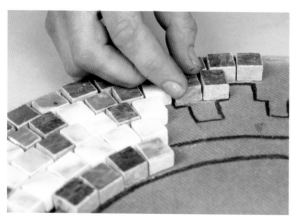

2 I Lay the marble tesserae with the right side up and without glue to plan the design. Make sure you get the spacing right, because this is how the completed mosaic will appear. When you are happy with the result, use a weak, 70:30, mix of water and water-soluble white craft glue to stick the marble tiles to the paper. Once finished, set aside to dry.

3 I Place the second sheet of paper on a flat surface and coat thoroughly with a stronger solution of water and water-soluble white craft glue—40:60. It is vital that the paper is covered completely: any gaps will cause the mosaic to fall apart. Work quickly so the paper does not have time to stretch.

4 I Place the glue-coated paper on top of the mosaic, and press the paper flat on the polished face of the tiles.

5 I Moving quickly, sandwich the mosaic between two boards. Gripping both boards tightly, turn the sandwich over. Remove the upper board. Press the mosaic hard through the paper to ensure every piece has made contact with the glue-coated paper now on the bottom. Leave to dry.

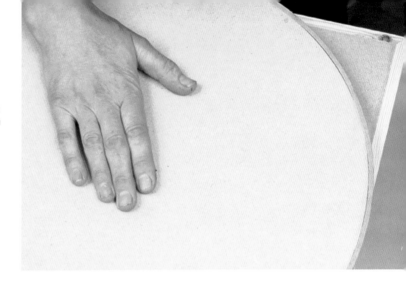

6 I Wet the top paper thoroughly with a moist but not dripping sponge. Leave for ten minutes, checking regularly to see if any paler patches have appeared. If so, rewet thoroughly, but do not use so much water that it soaks into the paper underneath. When the paper is saturated and has turned a dark brown, experiment with peeling it back. If there is some resistance, rewet. If not, peel it back (see Step 6 of Working indirectly on paper, page 127).

7 I Pre-grout the mosaic (see page 125). Prepare the substrate with the appropriate adhesive and seat the mosaic into it. To ensure the surface is flat and to eliminate any air pockets trapped between the layers of adhesive, tap over the mosaic with a small board and hammer or a float.

8 I Repeat Step 6 to wet and remove the remaining sheet of brown paper. While the adhesive is still wet, carefully sponge any remaining glue from the surface, working from the edge to the center so you do not move any tiles. Leave to dry, then grout from the front in the usual way (see page 30).

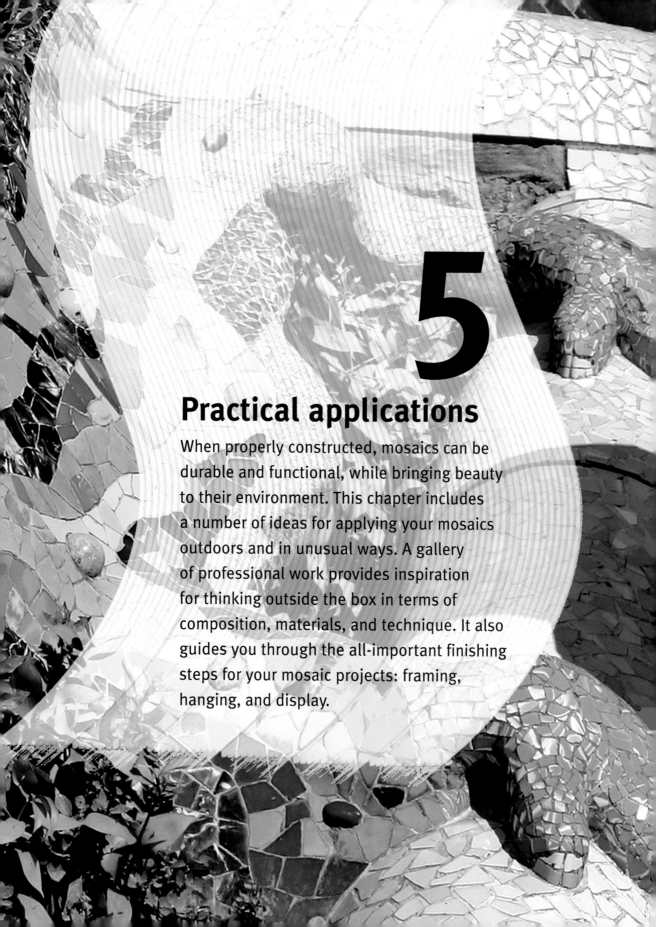

5

Practical applications

When properly constructed, mosaics can be durable and functional, while bringing beauty to their environment. This chapter includes a number of ideas for applying your mosaics outdoors and in unusual ways. A gallery of professional work provides inspiration for thinking outside the box in terms of composition, materials, and technique. It also guides you through the all-important finishing steps for your mosaic projects: framing, hanging, and display.

Outdoor ideas

The most important aspect of making mosaics to be sited outdoors is to be sure that the materials you plan to use can withstand the weather conditions. You can mix different materials, but do not try to use domestic wall tiles, or any other materials that are not intended for exterior use, otherwise the careful labor you put into making the mosaic will be wasted.

JARGON BUSTER ◆ SOFT-BODIED CERAMIC TILE

Tiles that have been fired at low temperatures are not water-resistant, making them unsuitable for freeze/thaw cycles.

JARGON BUSTER ◆ HARD-BODIED CERAMIC TILE

Tiles that have been fired in the kiln at very high temperatures. They are water-resistant and can be used in constantly wet and exterior freezing conditions.

271

Exterior substrates

It is essential that an exterior mosaic be constructed on a weather-appropriate surface. The most cost-effective choices are marine-grade plywood, available from lumber yards, and tile backer board, which can be bought from a building supplier or home-improvement superstore. If weight is a concern, other products are available, including one composed of lightweight Styrofoam encased in mesh and cement. You can also get fiberglass panels made of aluminum honeycomb enclosed by epoxy, which is waterproof and will not rust or corrode.

269

Exterior tesserae

Porosity is critical to using a tile outdoors, since porous tiles should not be used outdoors where weather produces freeze/thaw cycles. Porosity classifications are impervious (least absorbent), vitreous, semivitreous, and nonvitreous (most absorbent).

Above: Garden gazing balls, such as this one by Kyra Bell, are fun and will liven up any garden. Appropriate substrates for gazing balls include bowling balls, inflatable balls covered in alkaline-resistant mesh and thinset, and polystyrene balls, also covered with alkaline-resistant mesh and thinset. Be sure to match your substrate with the appropriate adhesive.

267

Exterior adhesives

For exterior use choose thinset, silicone, or MAC glue. Most professional tile setters will tell you to only use thinset, which has been around in some form since the Roman Empire, and those mosaics are still with us!

268

Weatherproof materials

Pebbles and shells are ideal for outdoor mosaics because they are unaffected by the weather. Stained glass, glass tiles, and smalti are also good choices.

270

Indoors out

The double direct and indirect working methods (see pages 117–121 and 124–129) are ideal for large pieces that you plan to site outside. Using these techniques you can create your mosaic inside, without worrying about weather conditions.

This mailbox base by Bonnie Fitzgerald was made on a flat surface in the studio using the double direct on mesh technique. The design wraps all four sides, making a playful statement.

272
Birdbaths

Birdbaths are beautiful garden additions. Remember that its purpose is to allow birds to safely bathe, so choose tesserae that are flat and safe for them. Also, birds can be dirty, so think about using a gray grout rather than white.

This birdbath by Susannah Dryden was made over an existing concrete form purchased at a garden center. The stained glass sparkles in the sun.

FIX IT

273 **Bring the white back**
White grout is often favored for garden decor projects, but it can easily get dirty (everything from rain to pollution to soil). A quick and easy cleanup is to use bleach in a spray bottle, which brightens white grout right up.

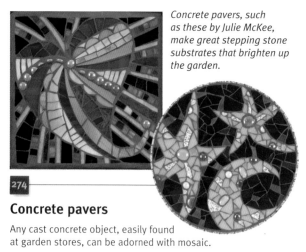

Concrete pavers, such as these by Julie McKee, make great stepping stone substrates that brighten up the garden.

274
Concrete pavers

Any cast concrete object, easily found at garden stores, can be adorned with mosaic.

275
Garden bench

Garden benches make great outdoor projects, but beware of sharp edges or pointed shards on seating areas. Consider using mosaic as a surface enhancement on vertical areas rather than the horizontal seating area.

This bench by Bonnie Fitzgerald originally featured a decorative ironwork-adorned back rest. This was removed and a suitable substrate cut to fit the gap, which was then covered in mosaic.

276
Water features

Mosaic water features are wonderful additions to any outside area, but beware of efflorescence (mineral deposits) and algae growth. Efflorescence can be removed using sulfuric acid crystals and hot water, and there are grout additives available that can help on both fronts.

277
Terracotta pots

Terracotta pots are great objects to mosaic, but beware, they are not usually rated freeze/thaw and can not be left outside in those climates. However, they make wonderful substrates and you can use glass, ceramic, or found object tessare.

Right: *Mosaic pots by Julie McKee. Remember to bring them in before the snow!*

Left: *Bonnie Fitzgerald's fountain is designed as a stylized trout stream and features three bas-relief spouting fish.*

Outdoor project: Shell flower trough

This piece utilizes found objects—in this case shells, pebbles, and broken mirror glass—direct set into a thinset suitable for outdoor use—one that is strong, waterproof, and, if you are in a cold climate, also frost resistant. You need to plan your work carefully in advance to ensure that you place your tesserae right the first time. The adhesive will set relatively quickly, so aim to complete one small area at a time.

7 1/2in (19cm)

8in (21cm)

19in (29cm)

7 1/2in (19cm)

Scale the design (see page 78–79) and use your scale drawing or printout to plan your design.

▲ **1** ▎ Sort the shells and pebbles by size, color, and type, using trays that have compartments so that you can separate the materials. This allows you to easily select the correct elements when working under the time pressure that drying thinset imposes.

You will need

Selection of shells and pebbles

Mirror tiles

Terracotta tiles

Grease pencil

Tile nippers

Thinset

Grouting squeegee or palette knife

▲ **2** ▎ Draw the design to size on a large piece of paper or cardboard, and tape it to a flat work surface where it will not be bumped—it's very easy to undo all your careful work in a second's clumsiness. Lay out the shells and stones on top of the drawing. Cut the mirror tiles with tile nippers and lay these out also. When you are happy with the dry run, position the trough close to the drawing so you can easily move the mosaic pieces between the two.

278

Sourcing shells

Collecting shells from beaches is not advisable for two reasons: first, it may be illegal to remove them, and second, you are unlikely to find the quantity and consistency that you require to match them closely by size and color. It is far better to buy them from specialist shell shops; there are countless distributors online.

▼ **3 |** Use a grease pencil to outline the design on the trough. This is only a rough guide since it will be covered with thinset, but it will serve as a guide when you apply the thinset in sections.

▲ **4 |** Work on distinct, small sections at a time, matching areas of the design. Starting in the center of the design, use a squeegee or palette knife to smear thinset on the center heart motif. You can roughly clear away excess using an old knife. The thinset needs to be laid on thick enough to hold the individual shells but not so thick that your tesserae get lost.

◀ **5 |** Working quickly, begin applying the shells by pressing them right into the thinset. Make an outline of white shells a little way in from the edge of the adhesive to establish the heart shape. Press in another inner row of shells to strengthen the shape.

▶ **6 |** Now fill in the heart with a crazy paving of cut mirror tiles. Press these pieces in firmly to submerge any sharp edges well below the level of the surrounding shells.

279

Make a prototype

If this is your first attempt at this type of project, it is worth practicing the adhesive and shell application on a small flat surface or a small pot. You need to press the objects into the adhesive so that they hold, but not so deep that they are submerged. Work neatly and get comfortable with the process before committing time and expense on the large version.

◀ **7 |** Add an outline of darker shells, to give the heart definition, and position larger shells around the top of the heart. With this section complete, you can now apply thinset to the area to the left of the heart (but leaving the top and bottom borders for now).

 280

Fill them up

A good tip for the larger shells is to fill them with some thinset and back butter them before pressing them into the adhesive on the pot. This not only strengthens them, but will help them to adhere better.

 281

Know your working time

Most thinset has a working time of approximately 30 minutes, so only apply it to an area you know you can complete in that time. If your thinset begins to dry out before you have set your tesserae, you will need to scrape it off and reapply.

▲ **8 |** Start with the shells that snake around the next section of the design, then fill in with the pebbles, making sure you press them in well, since they are heavy in comparison to the shells.

▶ **9 |** Fill up the design, pushing in the shells and pebbles as closely together as possible. Try to crowd each area, minimizing the amount of adhesive that remains visible. Repeat the design of this section, as closely as possible, as a mirror image on the right-hand side of the heart, working in exactly the same order.

▲ **10 ❙** Lastly, apply a thick border of thinset along the top edge of the trough and press in a row of rectangular or square mirror pieces. Again, try to submerge the sharp edges below the adhesive. Repeat this border along the bottom edge.

282
What you see is what you get

The need to work neatly is especially relevant with this project, since you will not be applying grout over the adhesive. The thinset you apply will be there forever, so make sure it is where you want it, and not somewhere you don't want to see it

FIX IT

283 At the end of the day
If you do not complete setting all of your tesserae in one sitting, be sure to clean up areas of unused thinset. Remember that this is a concrete project and once the thinset cures it will be impossible to remove.

▶ **11 ❙** Leave the first side to dry, then prop the trough up on its end and repeat the laying of the central heart motif exactly as before. Again leave to cure, then repeat on the other end. The shells are delicate, so to finish the opposite sides of the piece you will need to rest the side you have already completed on an old towel or rag to cushion the surface.

▶ If you will be using the trough in the garden or as a window box, you may not need to repeat the design on the back. Again, if you do, pad the bottom well, and avoid leaning or placing any weight on the pot. Find a home for the completed trough where it is not at risk of being knocked or damaged.

Templates: Flowers, foliage, and fruit

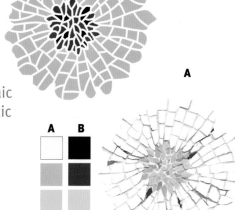

Flowers, leaves, and trees have always influenced mosaic design. They can be represented in a natural and realistic way, or be simplified and stylized until they become almost abstract. A beautiful flower can be the main subject of an artwork, or play the role of a decorative, additional element. Leaves and vines can integrate into borders and give a sense of movement to an otherwise static composition.

284

Stylized flower ▶

The tesserae that make up this stylized flower mosaic have been prettily shaped into individual petals, and the overall shape looks a little like a small fire with leaping flames. There is more variety of color among the petals in the variation; a warm color at the heart contrasts with many different blues.

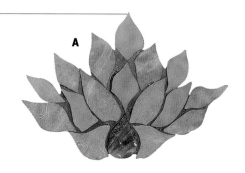

285

Daisy ▲

The yellow grout used in this daisy mosaic gives it a charming, pollen-dusted appearance, and helps to unify the petals and the yellow center. Daisies come in many sizes and colors, and the alternative "hot" version features orange petals and a dark center, that could be matched with a reddish grout.

286

Approaching flora

Flower designs can be simple or complex, and how you approach a flower mosaic is a matter of personal preference. The flower structure includes the petals, stigma, stamen, stem, and leaf. Do you want to incorporate those dimensions in your design or work in a flat, graphic manner? Either approach is fine, and a question of your own aesthetic.

287

Flower border ▼

This border mosaic is based on a busy little row of flowers. The idea is simple, but the many colors ensure that there is a lot going on in this design to interest the eye. The alternation of types of flower provides some consistency, as does the solidity of the background pattern, opus tessellatum. The alternative colorway makes use of a greater tonal contrast.

A

A   B

B

289

Falling leaf ▼

This leaf mosaic has a lovely jaunty curve to it, with a winding inner shape reminiscent of an oak leaf. Note how the first line of pale tesserae that surrounds this inner shape faithfully follows it around. The result is very decorative. The dark part of the rim defines the main shape, and balances well with the deep blue-green inner shape, while the red stem adds an intriguing glint. The variation suggests a more autumnal color scheme.

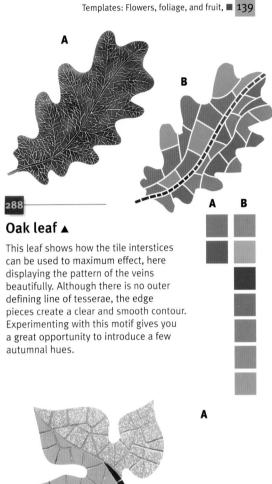

288

Oak leaf ▲

This leaf shows how the tile interstices can be used to maximum effect, here displaying the pattern of the veins beautifully. Although there is no outer defining line of tesserae, the edge pieces create a clear and smooth contour. Experimenting with this motif gives you a great opportunity to introduce a few autumnal hues.

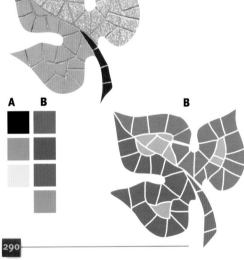

A   B

290

Vine leaf ▲

The popularity of the vine motif goes back to the Roman era, and it often crops up in ancient Roman floor mosaics. The shape of the leaf, with its deep curves, needs careful construction and individual cutting. The coloring of the original has an autumnal feel, but you could also employ summery greens.

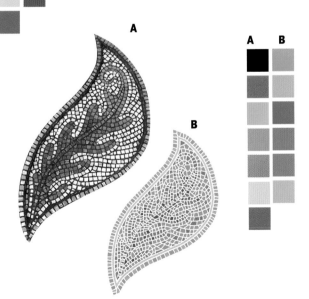

A   B

A   B

291

Tall palm ▶

Three different patterns make up this palm tree: the leaves, the coconuts, and the trunk. In each the tesserae have been specially shaped; the overall effect is rich and ornamental. Although the colors do not vary a great deal tonally, the green of the leaves is complementary to the reddish browns of the rest of the tree. This adds visual interest and balance. The variation suggests a palm tree at sunset, with deep, dark hues.

A

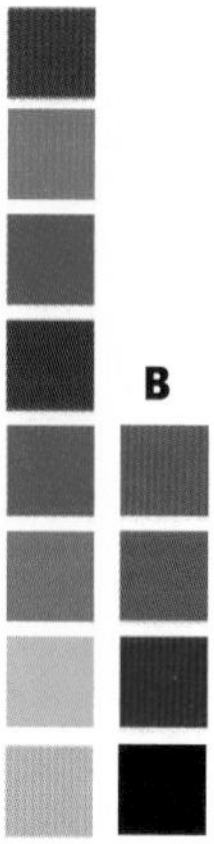

A

B

B

292

Inspiration

Fruit provides much scope for decorative motifs in mosaic: lovely rounded shapes, varied colors, and interesting patterns can be exploited when the fruit is cut open.

A

B

A

293

Fruit tree ▲

The leaves on this tree are all individually cut lozenges, and they have been informally laid to create a natural, leafy effect. The tree appears to be on fire: on one side the leaves are green and the trunk is brown, on the other the tree is blackened and charred and red flames are taking hold. The variation has orange leaves and blue flames scattered throughout (like a gas fire).

A

B

294

Swaying tree ◄

Trees can be adapted in many ways as mosaic images. This one has been given quite a plain color treatment, but the main interest lies in the andamento, which is full of movement and suggestive of billowing leaves swaying in the breeze. This design also offers great potential for mingling several colors, to give the impression of leaves fluttering and catching the light. Possible color variations include a fall version.

A   B

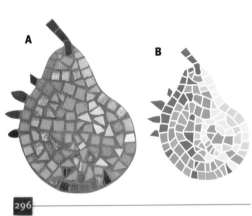

A

B

A   B

296

Pear ▲

An imaginative variety of colors is combined in this mosaic to produce a characterful piece of fruit. Note how the single tile outline creates a strong contour defining the beautiful pear shape, while the interior tesserae fill the space with a kind of organized chaos. The pattern, opus palladianum, is directionless in itself, but the colors work their way across the pear to create a definite progression: from the orangey reds on the one side to the light blues and greens on the other. The variation suggests an unripe pear in shades of green.

A

295

Pineapple

The spiky leaves and full, rounded shape of this pineapple mosaic are very convincing, and the use of turned, square tesserae is particularly successful in building up the diagonal pattern of the skin. The suggested variation takes a toned-down approach.

A   B

B

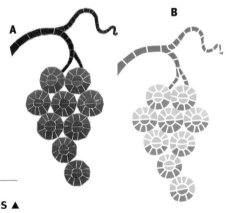

A   B

297

Bunch of grapes ▲

Light appears to be falling from above onto this bunch of grapes, because each mosaic grape is tonally graded to imply this. The bunch as a whole becomes darker at the bottom where there is less light. Naturally, grapes are found in some wonderful colors, and the alternative suggestion is a fresh green bunch, with the color of the stem providing a contrast.

Palette

 Clear   Peach

Gold   Light blue

Dark blue   Pale green

Red

You will need

Floating frame

Painter's or masking tape

Epoxy glue

Felt-tip pens

White paper

Tracing paper

Stained glass

Wheel cutters

MAC glue and gluing tools

Grout and grouting tools

Glass on glass project: Stained glass window hanging

This is a fun stained-glass project for artists of any experience level. Our example uses relatively large pieces of glass, but you can work in any scale you wish. Pattern ideas can be found online, or design your own. The window hanging is built using a floating frame—which can be purchased at most craft stores—so your work is framed as part of the making process. Your design can be as simple or complex as you wish, and you will enjoy the beauty of stained glass as the sun streams through the "window," casting magical colors all around.

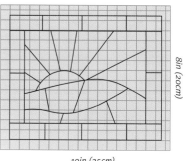

8in (20cm)

10in (25cm)

To scale and transfer the design, follow the techniques described on pages 78–79.

▲ **1 |** Most floating frames have two panes of glass. Remove one sheet of glass and keep the enclosed hardware for use later. You will need the frame, one sheet of glass, and the frame spacer.

TRY IT

298 **Wax paper**
If you don't have tracing paper, use kitchen wax paper as a substitute.

▲ **3 |** Use quick-setting epoxy glue to fix one sheet of glass to the inside of the frame, then glue the frame spacer to the inside of the frame on top of the glass (counter frame). Set aside to dry. Don't worry if the epoxy glue oozes onto the front of the glass, because it will be covered by your stained-glass artwork.

▲ **2 |** Cover the frame with painter's or masking tape to protect it from the adhesive.

▲ **4** ┃ Prepare your design and use felt-tip pen and white paper to make a pattern to fit the frame. Make a copy of the pattern on tracing paper. Tape the tracing-paper pattern to the back of the glass: the tracing paper will enable you to see how the glass will look with the sun shining through.

▲ **5** ┃ Working from the center of the design, begin cutting your glass to fit the pattern. Lay your glass over the pattern and trace the shape you wish to cut with a felt-tip pen. Use the appropriate tool to cut your glass into the desired shapes.

299

Light and dark

When using transparent stained glass, with the intention of having light pass through it, very dark grout works best. The dark, opaque grout lines force the light to do its very best work and intensify the glass colors and textures.

▲ **6** ┃ Position the dry-laid pattern next to your glass substrate and apply a generous amount of MAC glue to a manageable area of the design.

▲ **7** ┃ Glue the stained-glass elements in place, using the tracing-paper pattern under the glass to guide you. Keep your grout lines open with the aid of a stir stick. You do not need to glue the whole piece in one sitting, but MAC glue is a little runny, so make sure you clear the grout lines before resting. When the mosaic is complete, allow to dry overnight.

JARGON BUSTER ◆ CATHEDRAL GLASS
A term sometimes used to refer to transparent stained glass.

▼ ▶ Complete the project by grouting. Remove the tape from the frame and allow the grout to cure for a day or two before installing the hanging hardware.

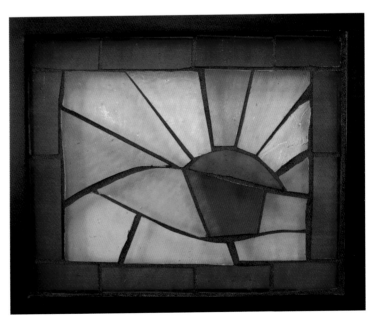

Finishing and fixing

The overall impression of a mosaic can be spoiled if the work is not finished to a high standard, so taking the time to finish and hang a mosaic well should be considered as important as the process of creating the piece in the first place. Finishing and fixing techniques are not only matters of presentation, however, they are also essential for protecting your mosaic from the elements, wear and tear, and accidental damage.

300
Buff

Always buff up a completed mosaic with a dry cloth. It is surprising how easy it is not to clean a mosaic properly. Sometimes it is difficult to see whether or not all the grout has been removed, particularly when the tiles are dark in color. The cloth abrades any film of grout left on the surface, and leaves the mosaic shiny and clean. The only exception to this is unglazed ceramic, which must be cleaned with water during the fixing process, because it will not rub clean later on.

301
Paint

Paint the sides and backs of completed mosaics. It is more sensible to do this before the mosaic is fixed, although you will probably need to retouch the paint once the mosaic is completed. Give as much thought to the paint color as you gave to the color of the tiles, because it will set off the appearance of the completed work, especially if your edges are visible.

302
Mosaic your mosaic!

An interesting finishing option is to mosaic the edges of your decorative mosaic artwork. If the work will not be manhandled, then tiling the edges of an artwork can not only give the impression of completion, but can be a fun design element.

Protect your surfaces

Protect your walls or table tops by covering the back of your smaller mosaics with a piece of felt, either the self-adhesive kind or stuck with PVA glue. Felt can be purchased at most craft stores.

Clean the natural way

A 50:50 mixture of white vinegar and water makes a great cleaning solution for mosaic surfaces, and removes most residue.

Frame your artwork

Framing your finished artwork not only says "I am done," but also "this is a work of art." Frames designed for paintings called "floating frames," because the canvas "floats" inside it, also make great frames for your mosaics. They can be found at most custom frame stores, or search for framing companies online.

Instant frame

Buy frames at yard sales and thrift stores. Cut a substrate to fit and you have an instant, inexpensive, frame.

Frame table tops

A good way to finish a table top is to attach a copper or stainless steel strip to the outside of the substrate to act as a frame. The frame must not extend higher than the level of the fixed mosaic, otherwise it will catch against things you place on the table. Use brass pins to attach the strip, since they will not rust, then grout the junction between the mosaic and the frame.

308

Hanging hardware

There are two parts to the process of hanging your finished mosaic: mounting hardware on the frame or substrate, and mounting the frame on the wall.

For the wall, you will either use a nail—which you will hammer right into the drywall or into a stud—a drywall anchor, or a picture hook.

There are more options for the frame hardware. The method you ultimately choose for both parts will depend upon several variables, including the size and weight of the artwork and the surface you will be hanging the artwork on.

309

Back to the start

Whenever possible, install your hanging and mounting devices before creating your mosaic, eliminating the probability of damaging your finished work. Some substrates actually require you to install the hanging hardware in advance (see Plan ahead, page 20), so always follow the manufacturer's instructions.

310

Hanging small or light mosaics

Using screw eyes or D-rings and wire are common ways to hang most two-dimensional artwork. Be sure the screw portion of the screw eye is not longer than your substrate and that the wire is pulled tight when you first install the hanging device. Over time the weight of the mosaic will stretch the wire. The wire manufacturer will give suggested weight limits. If you have had your mosaic professionally framed, it should already have a hanging wire.

Sawtooth picture hangers work well for lightweight mosaics and are easily installed, but not recommended for anything large or dimensional.

311

Hanging a large mosaic

For larger pieces, it is advisable to use a cleat system. Cleats are interlocking brackets designed for flush-mounting canvas art and open-back frames. The interlocking brackets provide safety and security and are advisable for works of any significant weight. These can be purchased online and at most home stores that carry framing hardware. You can also make a cleat by cutting a piece of wood lengthwise on a miter saw.

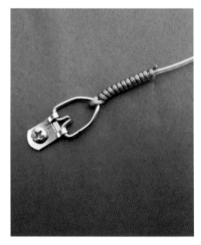

312

Specialty substrates may need specialty hanging devices

Wediboard needs to be hung using a special washer and screw system. The washer punctures the surface of the Wediboard, a corresponding washer is placed on the other side, and a hole is made in the center of the washer so a flat-head screw can be used to mount the mosaic flush on the wall. If you wish to hang the mosaic like a framed picture then a D-ring can be attached to the back of the washer and picture wire added.

313

Hanging a heavy mosaic

If the artwork is heavy, or you are unable to nail into a stud, an anchor system and screw may be a better choice for the wall. You must first drill a hole into the wall and insert the anchor into the hole. Then twist the screw into the anchor. The anchor keeps the screw in place and makes for a strong hold. If the work is to be sited outside, be sure to use a galavanized screw and plastic anchor.

FIX IT

314 **I've changed my mind**
Even though you are "sure" your mosaic will not need to be moved, just in case, it is a good idea to take a photograph of the piece and mark on it where you "hid" the screws. This way, if you do change your mind, you can simply pry off the relevant tesserae for unscrewing, without damaging the rest of the work. Of course, don't forget where you put the photograph!

316

Use studs for support

Make sure your wall can support your mosaic. Whenever possible, try to use the studs in the wall for additional support. Most constructions have studs every 16in (40cm). By hanging your nail on the wall side of a cleat into a stud you will have added support and structure. An easy way to find the studs is to use a stud finder.

FIX IT

317 **Balance is key**
Measure carefully to ensure that your fixings are placed an even distance from each side of the piece. If they are unevenly placed, it will be difficult to get the piece to hang straight.

315

Hidden mounting

When you are sure your mosaic will not need to be moved, you can use a hidden mounting method that fixes the mosaic in place permanently. This is also a good choice for large pieces. You need to have planned ahead for this method, since the first step is taken before the mosaic-making begins.

1 I Drill holes in the corners of the substrate before you begin applying your tesserae, countersinking the holes so that the screws will be level with the surface of the board. Leave the holes exposed, but tile and grout the rest of the piece.

2 I Mount the mosaic on the wall using flat-headed screws and an appropriate anchoring system.

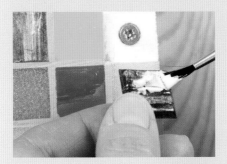

3 I When in place, glue down the missing tesserae pieces to cover the screw heads.

4 I When the glue has set, grout the new tiles in the same way as the rest of the mosaic.

Thinking outside the box

Artists find inspiration and express themselves in a variety of ways. Mosaic artists are no different. Sometimes art makes a statement, or tells a story. Other times art expresses emotions, or touches yours. Other art is there just because it was fun to make, and the process in and of itself is the art. Materials often guide mosaic artists; in cutting and fitting their tesserae, they often push the materials beyond expectations. The following pages are a snapshot of contemporary, fine-art mosaics. May they inspire you to think out of the box on your mosaic journey.

318

Cut and arrange your tesserae in unexpected ways

In *Red Moon Rising*, artist Kelley Knickerbocker used stained glass in two unusual ways: she stacked layers of stained glass on top of each other—creating a vibrant, three-dimensional effect—and she positioned some of the glass tesserae on their sides—exposing the striated, riven edge of the glass. The work is mesmerizing and dramatic. Materials: stained glass, 24k gold. Size: 10 x 10in (25 x 25cm)

319

Embrace design principles

Sherri Warner Hunter wanted to emphasize the importance of line quality by using a found piece of wood and the placement of the small tiles in this piece, *Little Bean*. The lines created with the ceramic tesserae wrap around the bean shape drawing the viewer's eye around and then up the branch. The branch for *Little Bean* was in her studio for over five years, waiting for the right concept to come to mind. Materials: concrete over polystyrene, porcelain tile, wood. Size: 2ft 2in x 1ft 2in x 5in (66 x 36 x 13cm)

 320

Look to the cosmos

The Hubble Telescope has captured extraordinary images, allowing us to witness the most spectacular and mysterious depths of the universe; Bonnie Fitzgerald was inspired by these images in *Merging Galaxies*. The andamento of the tesserae create a sense of order in the exploding chaos, but the vastness of space is conveyed through using black stained glass and black grout for the background. Materials: vitreous glass tiles, stained glass, 24K gold. Size: 36 x 48in (90 x 120cm)

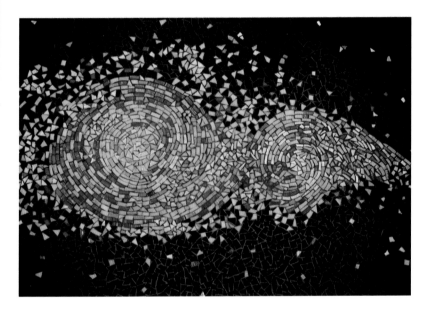

321

Find an anchor element

Anchor elements are things that dominate a mosaic work. An anchor will ideally be combined with supporting materials that showcase its personality. In this piece, *Day One: The Birth of Light*, by Bill Buckingham, the fluorate anchor is beautifully set off by the other materials and grounds the work's radiating energy. Materials: fluorate, selenite, mica, marble, granite, onyx, aventurine, gypsum, sodalite, meteorites. Size: 25 x 16in (63 x 40cm).

322

Color your thoughts

In *Thinking*, Carol Shelkin captured mood and sensitivity using an unconventional color palette. Taking advantage of the unique patterning in stained glass she created a deeply emotional work. The stained-glass tesserae are cut in odd shapes, yet they perfectly fit together to create a unified and realistic portrait. There is a subtle whimsy to the work because of the color palette. Materials: stained glass. Size: 12 x 12in (30 x 30cm).

323

Be inspired by your own story

In this playful mixed-media sculpture, *Conjure Woman*, artist Lori Greene drew inspiration from her ethnic heritage: African and Native American (Mississippi Choctaw). The handmade armature is embellished with traditional mosaic materials as well as tiny beads—these create a rich texture, delightful patterns, and pops of color. Materials: china, beads, ceramic, viterous glass. Size: 17 x 6 x 6in (43 x 15 x 15cm).

324

Create texture

In *Owl's Eye*, by Michele Falvo, the stained-glass tesserae were cut into brushstroke-shaped pieces and layered to depict the delicate feathers circling the eye. Added visual texture is created by mixing the colors of the "brushstrokes" and using the striations in the glass. Materials: stained glass. Size: 12in x 12in (30 x 30cm).

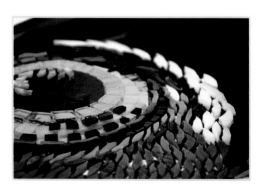

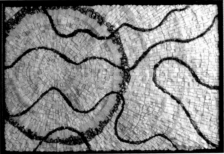

325

Beauty can be subtle

In *Wired*, artist Carol Talkov takes the hard surface of marble and by exposing the crystallized interior of the stone, she reveals the soft beauty inside. The undulating substrate gives the impression that the stone is more flexible than its actual nature. Materials used: carrara marble, black tourmaline, selenite, optic calcite, pyrite. Size: 12 x 18 in (30 x 45 cm)

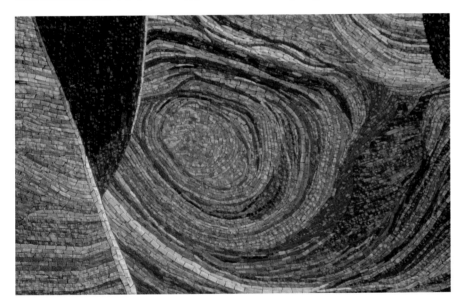

326

Look to the earth

This mosaic, *Timeless Vortex*, by Michael Welch, was inspired by the patterns found on the walls of Antelope Canyon, Arizona. The shapes are realistic as well as abstracted and the hues are quiet and bold at the same time. Materials: smalti. Size: 15 x 24in (38 x 60cm)

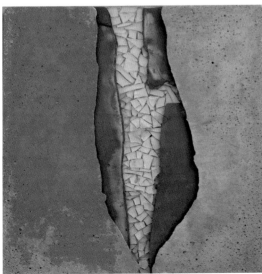

327

Mix up your materials and methods

Kim Wozniak is inspired by materials she has salvaged and treasured and is motivated by breaking set ideas of what mosaics are. In this piece, *Cleavage*, she used materials not traditionally associated with mosaic-making (lightweight concrete) with more conventional ones (slate and tempered glass) that she had reclaimed. The piece is also constructed from traditionally laid tesserae combined with cast concrete. Materials: lightweight concrete, slate, and tempered glass. Size: 15 in x 15in (38 x 38cm).

Glossary

Adhesive
The various types of glue or cement-based products used to attach mosaic tesserae onto a substrate.

Andamento
The placement of tesserae in a flowing pattern to suggest movement and rhythm—the mosaic equivalent of a brushstroke.

Back-buttering
Applying adhesive to the back of tesserae pieces.

Ceramic tiles
Ceramic tiles are made from a layer or layers of fired clay. Available in a wide range of textures and colors, they are a popular mosaic material. Ceramic tiles can be easily cut and shaped using standard hand tools including tile cutters and tile nippers.

Direct set
Mosaics with tesserae set into a bed of mortar and not grouted. This is most common when working with smalti and found object tesserae.

Direct method
The mosaic method by which tesserae are laid and affixed directly onto a final surface.

Dry lay
The process of laying tesserae in place without adhesive, for planning purposes.

Glass scorer
The scoring tool has a small carbide wheel at one end. The wheel is either dragged or pushed along the glass surface thus breaking the surface tension. The glass is then snapped apart with a runner.

Grout
A cement-based product mixed with water to produce a paste which fills the space (interstices) between tiles/tesserae. Used to both decorate and stabilize the work, grout has no adhesive properties.

Grout joint
Also referred to as a "grout line," this is the space left between tiles/tesserae that is filled with grout.

Indirect method
Also called "reverse method," a fabrication technique whereby a mosaic is developed in reverse onto a temporary surface before being turned over and permanently affixed into place.

Interstices
The space between laid tesserae on a mosaic. This space may either be grouted or not depending on the desired design outcome.

Mastic
A premixed ceramic tile adhesive.

Millefiori
Literally "thousand flowers" in Italian, this term refers to small tesserae created by the fusion of many glass rods arranged so that the cross section creates a floral or geometric pattern. These rods are then sliced thinly and encased in glass.

Nippers
Plier-like hand tool used to cut, shape, or "nip" tile or glass. Rotary or wheel nippers have two carbide wheels used for glass and sometimes tile. Off-set tile nippers are used to cut or shape tile only.

Opus
This is the Latin word for "work." It describes the design, andamento, placement of tesserae, or flow of mosaic work. The plural of opus is "opera."

Opus circumactum
Laying of tesserae in a fan-like, circular pattern.

Opus musuvium
Tesserae outline the main features of the design and continue to flow outward, filling the entire background.

Opus palladianum
Laying of assorted shaped tesserae in a random, interlocking pattern. Also known as "crazy paving."

Opus regulatum
Laying of tesserae in a straight, gridlike pattern.

Opus sectile
Each tessera is cut to form a complete shape in itself.

Opus tesselatum
Laying of tesserae in a straight line on one axis, but with broken yet parallel lines on a second axis, like bricklaying.

Opus vermiculatum
Laying of tesserae in wavy lines, in a worm-like fashion.

Runner
Hand tool used to snap/break a score line on a piece of glass. Also known as running pliers

Slake
The chemical reaction that occurs when water is introduced and mixed with dry thinset mortar or grout.

Smalti
Tesserae formed from molten glass poured into patties, cooled, and cut into individual pieces. Extremely light-reflective, smalti are available in a tremendous range of colors.

Squeegee
A tool for spreading grout. The squeegee has a rubber blade on one edge that helps force the grout into all the spaces.

Stained glass
Thin glass that has been colored with the addition of metallic salts during its manufacture. It can be cut easily into desired shapes for mosaic. Iridescent stained glass has a metallic sheen, like oil on a glass surface.

Substrate
Any surface used as a base for a mosaic.

Tessellate
To repeat a pattern indefinitely without gaps or overlapping.

Tessera
The individual units that are used to make up a mosaic, including small bits of tile, glass, ceramic, stone, or other media. The plural of tessera is "tesserae."

Thinset mortar
A dry mix of Portland cement, sand, and sometimes latex additives used for bonding tesserae to a substrate. This adhesive is commonly required for use in exterior settings.

Tile nippers
A handheld tool used for breaking, snipping, and shaping mosaic materials such as vitreous glass tiles, ceramic tiles, or crockery.

Vitreous glass
A uniform manufactured glass tile made in molds from glass paste. These tiles have a smooth top and a rough, textured back.

Below: Coastal Reflections of Fort Walton Beach *by George Fischman*

Resources

Mosaic art organizations

**British Association for
Modern Mosaic (BAMM)**
www.bamm.org.uk

Contemporary Mosaic Art (CMA)
mosaicsandceramics.ning.com

**German Organization for
Mosaic Art (DOMO)**
www.domo-ev.de

**International Association of
Contemporary Mosaicists (AIMC)**
www.aimcinternational.com

**Mosaic Art Association in Japan
(MAAJ)**
hwww.maa-jp.com

**Mosaic Association of Australia
and New Zealand (MAANZ)**
www.maanz.org

**Mosaic Association
South Africa (MASA)**
mosaicassociationsa.ning.com

**Society of American
Mosaic Artists (SAMA)**
www.americanmosaics.org

Resource List

USA

Delphi Glass
www.delphiglass.com
800 248 2048

Diamond Tech
www.diamondtechcrafts.com
800 937 9593

diMosaico
www.dimosaico.com
866 437 1985

Ed Hoy Art Glass and Supplies
www.edhoy.com
800 323 5668

KP Tiles
www.kptiles.com
248 425 6291

Maryland Mosaics
www.marylandmosaics.com
410 702 7544

Monster Mosaics
www.monstermosaics.com
888 236 4001

Mosaic Basics
www.MosaicBasics.com
404 939 4892

Mosaic Mercantile
www.mosaicmercantile.com
877 966 7242

Mosaic Rocks!
www.mosaicrocks.com
800 983 4820

Mosaic Tools.com
www.mosaictools.com
800 557 3444

Mosaics by Maria
www.mosaicsbymaria.com
828 312 0291

MosaicSmalti
www.mosaicsmalti.com
866 432 5369

Rainbow Stained Glass
www.rainbowglassonline.com
215 785 3034

Smalti.com
www.smalti.com
888 494 8736

Tiny Pieces
www.tinypiecesmosaics.com
773 832 9410

Tiny Tile Mosaics
www.tinytilemosaics.com
843 821 1866

Warner Stained Glass
www.stained.com
800 523 4242

Wits End Mosaics
www.witsendmosaic.com
888 494 8736

Youghiogheny Glass
www.youghioghenyglass.com
724 628 3000

CANADA

Fantasy in Glass
www.fantasyinglass.com
416 252 6868

Mosaic Art Source
mosaicartsource.com

Mosaic Beach Studio
www.mosaicbeach.com
416 915 1627

Mosaïkashop
www.mosaikashop.com
514 582 7476

UNITED KINGDOM

DyeGrout
www.dyegrout.com
01795 871 972

Mosaic Direct
www.mosaic-direct.com
0771 312 3565

Mosaic Heaven
www.mosaicheaven.com
01778 380 989

Mosaic Supplies Ltd
www.mosaicsupplies.co.uk
01299 828 374

Mosaic to Fit
www.mosaictofit.co.uk
07814 408 413

Mosaic Trader
www.mosaictraderuk.com
01227 459 350

Opus Mosaic
www.opusmosaic.co.uk
01392 496 393

Tempsford Stained Glass
www.tempsfordstainedglass.co.uk
01767 640 235

The Mosaic Gallery
www.mosaicsonline.co.uk
01424 211 947

AUSTRALIA

Australian Stained Glass Supplies
www.asgs.com.au
02 9660 7444

Brett Campbell Mosaics
www.mosaics.com.au

Oz Mosaics
www.ozmosaics.com.au
07 3847 4873

Smalti Australia
www.smaltiaustralia.com
02 9940 0101

Specialty Art Glass
www.specialtyartglass.com.au
02 9940 0101

ITALY

Xinamarie Mosaici
www.xinamarie.com
0340 463 7731

Orsoni Smalti Veneziani
www.orsoni.com
0412 440 0023

NETHERLANDS

The Craft Kit
www.thecraftkit.com
0297 344 668

Tiles and Tools
www.tilesandtools.eu
0622 775 868

Right: Mosaic Quilt *by Bonnie Fitzgerald*

Index

Credits

Quarto would like to thank the following artists for kindly supplying images for inclusion in this book:

Bell, Kyra c/o www.maverickmosaics.com, pp.59br, *My Little Duckling*, photographer Kevin Maxson, 132bl, *Garden Orb "Blossom"*, photographer Bonnie Fitzgerald

Branningan, Colette, colettebrannigan. com, p.67t

Bryan, Ilona pp.65b, 66br

Buckingham, Bill www.mosaicrocks.com, p.149tl, *Day One: The Birth of Light*, photographer Bill Buckingham

Buxton, Joanna p.67bl

Catalano, Lia at Hannacrois Mosaics p.49t

Charnock, Stephen p.110b

Davidson, Mark p.49c

Dryden, Susannah c/o www. maverickmosaics.com, p.133t, *Birdbath*, photographer Bonnie Fitzgerald

Falvo, Michele c/o www.maverickmosaics. com, p.150b, *Owl's Eye*, photographer Brian Hoeg

Favagehi, Taraneh c/o www. maverickmosaics.com, p.95br, *Red and White*, photographer Kevin Maxson

Field, Robert, www.robert-field.co.uk, p.110tl

Fishman, George www. georgefishmanmosaics.com, pp.54bl, *Zippori*, photographer George Fishman, 87tr, *Vespucci*, photographer George Fishman, 152–152, *Coastal Reflections of Fort Walton Beach*, photographer Scott Marshall

Fitzgerald, Bonnie www. bonniefitzgeraldart.com, pp.28, *Spinning Nebula*, photographer Bonnie Fitzgerald, 31l, *Magic Mushroom*, photographer Kenneth Fitzgerald, 46l and 155, *Mosaic Quilt*, photographer Kenneth Fitzgerald, 54 t, *Potomac River Fish*, photographer Kenneth Fitzgerald, 98 br, *Pear Tree*, created in realism workshop with Shug Jones, photographer Kenneth Fitzgerald, 99t, *Pansy*, created in mosaic flower workshop with Yulia Hanansen, photographer Brian Hoeg, 116b, *Door Stoops and Lamp*, photographer Kenneth Fitzgerald, 118-119, *Hunters Woods Elementary School*, photographer (work in progress) Kenneth Fitzgerald, photographer (completed work) Katie Haynie, 132br, *Mailbox*, photographer Kenneth Fitzgerald, 133cr, *Garden Bench*, assisted by Maverick Mosaics staff, photographer Brian Hoeg, 133bl, *Trout Stream*, photographer Michael Barolet, 144br, *Form vs. Function*, photographer Kenneth Fitzgerald, 149c, *Merging Galaxies*, photographer Bonnie Fitzgerald

Kenneth Fitzgerald www. maverickmosaics.com, p.109tr, *Celtic Knot*, photographer Brian Hoeg

Kuo Kang Chen, p.11

Gardner, Virginia www.virginiamosaics. com, pp.72b, *Secrets*, photographer Bill Moretz, 74l, *Allure*, photographer Bill Moretz

Green, Lori www.greenemosaic.com, p.150t, *Conjure Woman*, photographer Usry Alleyne

Hankin, Tessa at Mosaics Workshop p.67br

Haslehurst, Nicola pp.48cl, 50br

Heisler, Rhonda www. rhondaheislermosaicart.com, pp.72t, *Autumn Leaves*, photographer Rhonda Heisler, 85b, *Encoded*, photographer Rhonda Heisler

Imbert, Sally pp.139bl, 140t, 140b, 141tr

King, Sonia www.mosaicworks.com, p.77b, *Nebula Aqua*, photographer Sonia King

Knickerbocker, Kelley www. rivenworksmosaics.com, p.148bl, *Red Moon Rising*, photographer Kelley Knickerbocker

Kozacheck, Janet p.65c

Letchford, Jo, www.joletchfordmosaics.co. uk, p.64b

Levy, Irit, iritlevymosaicart.blogspot.com, p.85tr, *Big Steps*, photographer Irit Levy

Mary-Kei Mosaics pp.50tr, 138tr, 141bl

Massey, Peter at Zantium pp.48b, 50tl, 51cr, 66cl, 67cr, 111br

Maxson, Jessica c/o www. maverickmosaics.com, p.31r, *Il Pavone*, created in a Byzantine mosaic workshop, Ravenna, Italy, photographer Kevin Maxson

McKee, Julie www.coastaltilearts.com, pp.2bl and 133cl, *Heart Garden Paver*, photographer Brian Hoeg, 133c, *Stars and Moon Garden Paver*, photographer Brian Hoeg, 133br, *Terracotta Pots*, photographer Brian Hoeg

Naumez, Wladimir at Mosaik, www. mosaicnaumez.com, p.51bl

Neville Smith, Melissa p.110tr

Newnham, Rebecca, www. rebeccanewnham.co.uk, p.139t

Prunti, Elaine at Imago Mosaic, www. elaineprunty.com, p.138c,

Sapwell, Clare p.50cl

Shapiro, Marian www.dariandesign.com. au, pp.85 tl, *Mosman*, photographer Marian Shapiro, 124 bl, *Jellyfish Floor Medallion*, photographer Marian Shapiro

Shelkin, Carol www.carolshelkinmosaics. com, pp.83, *Becoming*, photographer Carol Shelkin, 149b, *Thinking*, photographer Carol Shelkin

Shreve Taylor, Andrea www.taylormosaics. com, pp.36br, *Road Hog*, photographer Brian Hoeg, 54br, *Sammy*, photographer Brian Hoeg

Stewart Smith, Jeni pp.64t, 66t

Suplita, Barbara www. barbarasuplitamosaics.com, p.143, *Sunrise*, photographer Kenneth Fitzgerald

Talkov, Carol www.studiocwebsite.com, pp.2tr, *Old Blue Eyes*, created in Layered Technique workshop with Yulia Hanansen, photographer Kenneth Fitzgerald, 151t, *Wired*, photographer Kevin Maxson

Thevenot, Michael p.65t

Wates, Rosalind pp.48tr, 49b, 51t, 111t, 111cl, 139br, 141tl, 141br

Warner Hunter, Sherri www. sherriwarnerhunter.com, p.148tr, *Little Bean*, photographer Sherri Warner Hunter

Welch, Michael www.mosaicrocks.com, p.151c, *Timeless Vortex*, photographer Michael Welch

Wozniak, Kim www.kimwozniak.com, p.151b, *Cleavage*, photographer Kim Wozniak

Alejandro Mozo p.10cr, Christopher Elwell p.10t, Coprid 12tr, Courtyardpix p.138b, 140b, David H.Seymour p.103tr, De2marco p.146tc, Defpicture p.68–69, Dmitry Melnikov p.29tc, Feng Yu p.27cl, Hsagencia p.29tr, Irina Fischer p.19tr, J

van der Wolf p.73tr, Jcjgphotography p.147cl, Mackey Creations 13, Maxim Tupikov p.112–113, Mircea Bezergheanu p.39tl, Mirka Moksha p.24br, Mountainpix p.73tl, Nodff p.75t, Olena Mykhaylova p.24cl, rSnapshotPhotos p.39bl, Rynio Productions p.17br, Smirnov Maksim p.146br, Taelove7 14cl, Tratong p.8–9, Vadim Kozlovsky p.24tr, Vasiliy Koval/ MarFot/Andrey Tirakhov p47b, Wh Chow p.73cr, 130-131, Zimmytws/Apollofoto/ Marie C Fields/Nito p.36bl: all from Shutterstock.com

Colevineyard p.32–33 from iStock.com

Some of the content in this book has also appeared in *50 Mosaic Murals*, *The Mosaic Artist's Bible*, *The Encyclopedia of Mosaic Techniques*, *Mosaic Basics/Start Mosaics*, *Mosaic Idea Book*, and *Mosaic Decorator's Sourcebook*.

The opportunity to put together this book was a gift made possible by my friend, mentor, and fellow mosaic artist Bill Buckingham. You are missed. A special thank you to my husband Ken and our daughter Stephanie who support every wild idea I have. And of course my thanks to the amazing staff and many friends of "Maverick" who all contribute their time and talents in countless ways to support our community. I am grateful to you. A special shout out to all my colleagues in the art community who continue to support and nurture my passion to express my creative voice.

Bonnie Fitzgerald